Prefabricated Systems

Principles of Construction

These titles have also been published in this series:

Maarten Meijs, Ulrich Knaack
Components and Connections – Principles of Construction
ISBN 978-3-7643-8669-6

Ulrich Knaack, Tillmann Klein, Marcel Bilow, Thomas Auer
Façades – Principles of Construction
ISBN 978-3-7643-7962-9

Ulrich Knaack
Sharon Chung-Klatte
Reinhard Hasselbach

Prefabricated Systems

Principles of Construction

Birkhäuser
Basel

We would like to thank Delft University of Technology for the financial support of this publication.
We would also like to thank Ria Stein for her editorial guidance and her prolonged efforts;
our thanks are extended to Sabine Kühnast for her competent support of our work.
Thanks are due to Pieter Moerland as well for his comments and to the research student
Christian Wedi for generating the drawings.

Layout and typesetting: MEDIEN PROFIS, Leipzig
Graphic design concept: Oliver Kleinschmidt, Berlin
Editor: Ria Stein, Berlin
Subject editor: Sabine Kühnast, Berlin
Copyediting (chapters 1, 2, 3, 7): Raymond Peat, Alford, Aberdeenshire
Translation into English (chapters 4, 5, 6): Raymond Peat, Alford, Aberdeenshire

This book is also available in a German edition:
978-3-7643-8746-4

A CIP catalogue record for this book is available from the Library of Congress,
Washington D.C., USA.

Bibliographic information published by the German National Library
The German National Library lists this publication in the Deutsche Nationalbibliografie;
detailed bibliographic data are available on the Internet at http://dnb.d-nb.de.

P.O. Box, 4009 Basel, Switzerland
Part of De Gruyter

Printed on acid-free paper produced from chlorine-free pulp. TCF ∞
Printed in Germany

ISBN 978-3-7643-8747-1

9 8 7 6 5 4 3 2 1
www.birkhauser.ch

CONTENTS

Appendix

1 | Introduction

Building with prefabricated systems encompasses the production and use of preplanned components or modules as a solution to build with higher quality and more efficiency. It is associated with dimensional grids, high technical standards, lower costs and the repetition of components or objects. Today, almost every science and industry is systemised, and the building industry is not an exception, but rather a late bloomer.

Building systems are used to simplify complex planning and constructional processes. Their special character lies in the fact that they are not related to any specific building task but can be applied as universal solutions. System building is often referred to as prefabricated systems because of the industrial nature of construction production. Many building systems consist of manufactured components and use industrial methods of assembly, even when constructed on site.

Terminology

The term system building must also be seen in the context of a time horizon. The first systematisations applied to the smallest units: bricks, which had been in use since 7500 BCE. Today's system building is relevant to much larger and more complex components.

The increasing complexity of systematisation is demonstrated by the term "module" (*modulus*, Latin for measure). Whereas in earlier times, module described standardised measurements or dimensions, such as the Japanese tatami mat or Le Corbusier's modulor, the term today stands for standardised components of an overall system. And the components can be further broken down into separate elements.

In the last century, visionary experiments in building systems enjoyed public attention, but the novelty of industrialisation wore off relatively quickly in architecture. The mass production of standard components is thriving, and in some sectors, such as housing, prefabrication of whole buildings is experiencing a slow restart.

A one-off product is still perceived as a handcrafted work of art, and the repetitive industrialised house does not conjure up images of the beautiful home. Is it impossible to create good architectural products and repeat them hundreds of times? Or is the dream of high-quality, cost-effectively produced architecture purely an ideological position that does not work in today's world of individualists? Is the element of prefabrication reciprocal with the idea of non-permanence, or is there too much hesitance in acquiring a high-tech product that is larger than an automobile and lasts for longer than ten years?

This leads to the question of good vs. bad architecture. Does serial production lower product value? Artists Andy Warhol and Dan Flavin based some of their works on the notion of repetition of identical everyday objects (1). The series of otherwise simple Campbell's soup cans or the marching rhythm of fluorescent light tubes is the essence of the artists' works. Can a repetitive built environment (2) be planned intelligently and provide the essence of architecture we are looking for? In the search for individuality and corporate identity, does mass customisation suffice in architecture?

Building systems and prefabrication

Taking a step back to the roots of the matter to inquire about the systematisation of architecture (4), we recognise that many architects and builders rely heavily on systems because the demands of the scope of the projects and the expected time of delivery cannot be met with traditional methods. Building systems include the production of building elements, whether on or off site; the subcategory prefabrication includes all systemised off-site manufacturing of components and elements (3). Among the benefits of successfully using systems, including prefabrication, are quicker construction on site, better ability to build to optimum cost and higher-quality end products due to closer factory control as part of the manufacturing process.

From an architect's point of view, the impact of prefabrication on architecture is positive on the one hand, because the profession consistently involves more areas of responsibility, and prefabrication allows a cumulative development of technical knowledge: connections, details and technical standards. On the other hand, it has a negative image because it instigates a fear that intelligent thinking and creative architecture, as well as the architectural profession itself, are becoming obsolete. From the clients' point of view, building systems have a reputation ranging from low construction standards to high-end technology and are even ultimately considered fashionable.

System building is generally believed to be the opposite of on-site building because the manufacturing takes place off site. It is not associated with anything organic: systemised building usually connotes boxy, orthogonal shapes and strict grids. The style of prefabricated systems scoffs at the sort of architecture that conjures the homemade aura, or the vernacular (of a place), since the industry and industrialised products aspire to speak a modern language (of a time). However, these generalisations are only partly correct.

1

Fluorescent light installation, Menil Collection, Richmond Hall, Houston, Texas, Dan Flavin, 1996
The repetition of elements, like the colourful fluorescent light tubes of this sculpture, constitutes a whole. A twin set bedecks the other side of the hall.

2

Prefabricated houses in Middelburg, the Netherlands
The individual façade is not of high priority on this Dutch street. The repetition of housing units unifies the street façade and demonstrates that the order of the repetitive built environment is a strong virtue.

On-site methods of construction, for example, stick-built houses, are often thought to be the slower, hand-made methods. In some cases, stick-built methods, have indeed become more systemised, methodically and architecturally, than prefab products on the market today. Some on-site building construction methods may be low-tech, but other on-site building procedures that parallel advanced high-efficiency production methods of the factory far exceed the production output of standard building procedures. Cases in point are Quadrant Homes of USA and Toyota Homes of Japan. Business management experts from the automobile industry who learned from each other overseas and constantly oversaw self-improvement plans are responsible for these highly efficient and successful building construction methods. Whereas Toyota Homes prefabricates the house components in the factory, the American firm produces most of the homes on site – and both produce stick-built homes at top speed and with admirable quality. Clearly, system building does not necessarily take place off site.

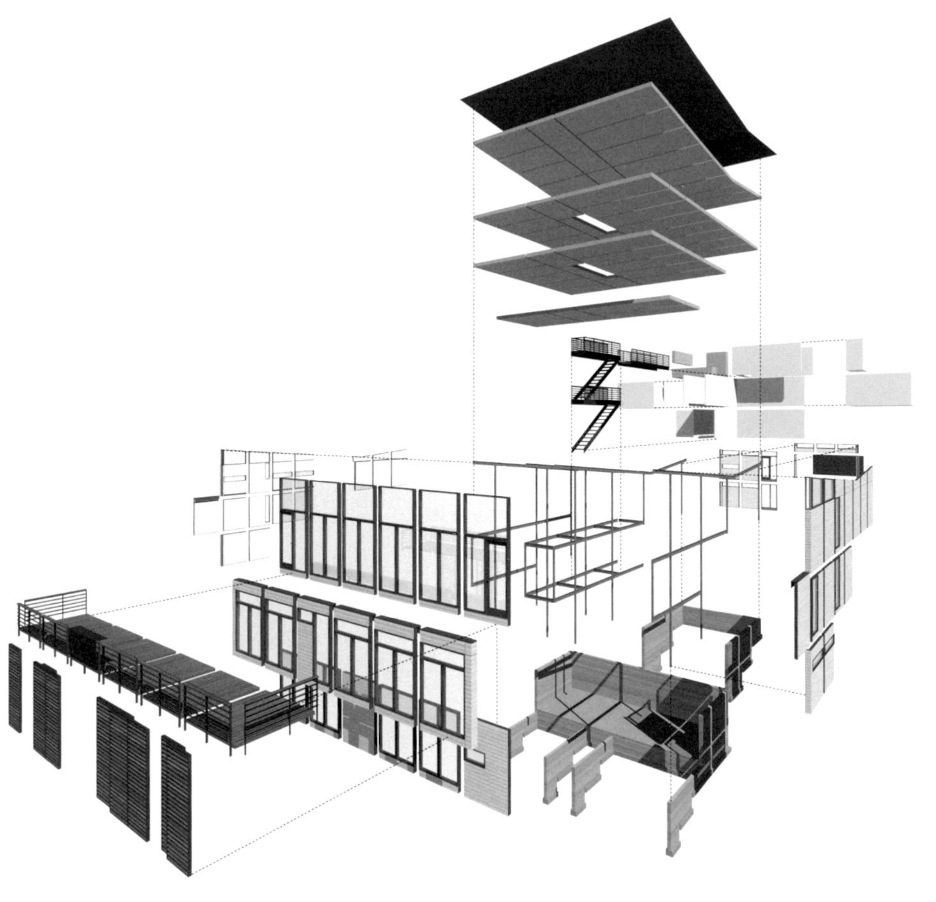

3

Parco Homes, San Francisco, California
Many prefabricated homes offer a variety of sizes and materials to suit the individual customer's needs. The exploded axonometric shows a prefabricated kit of parts that is assembled on site.

4

Islamic pattern, Alhambra, Granada
The geometry sets the order of the coordinates of all the lines, which interweave to form patterns. In the same way, building systems set the order of all subsystems and components to form a building.

Housing and industrial building

This book discusses two areas of construction that could hardly be more different: residential and industrial building. These areas were selected because they already have a particularly high degree of prefabrication and comprise a large proportion of total building activity.

Several factors shape the housing market: there are private clients, who favour individualisation but would still like to build cost-effectively and/or with a guarantee on price. This segment covers, among other things, prefabricated housebuilding companies, which, for example, claim 14 % of the market in Germany. On the other hand, real estate companies design and develop whole new residential areas, where there is a high demand for housing, such as in the Netherlands.

The industrial building category includes offices, commercial and industrial buildings, which have to fulfil a very wide range of different requirements. On the one hand there is the inner-city office block, which has to meet the architectural and urban-planning requirements and accommodate complex building services. And on the other hand, there are the factories and warehouses, which, because they are often erected on the urban periphery, have to satisfy much reduced needs for architectural expression and building services.

The architectural quality that can be achieved with preplanning and prefabrication must therefore be considered with respect to the particular project. With prefabrication can come loss of local typology, construction methods and materials. Other building types, for example stadia, can profit from a high degree of prefabrication and, as the contract sum is many times that of a single detached house, new designs can be developed exploring options for prefabrication and modularisation to form a project-specific modular building system.

5

Soccer City Stadium, Johannesburg, Boogertman + Partners, 1987/2010
2,100 modules, each consisting of 16 panels in various colours and surface finishes, create a shape reminiscent of the African calabash.

6

Soccer City Stadium, Johannesburg
Glass fibre-reinforced concrete façade modules supplied by the German company Rieder were used for the roof of the stadium, which was built in 1987. Detailed view of installation.

Today, system-built products can even assume organic shapes (5, 6, 9). Moulding of three-dimensional forms, calibrating movements and translating information for CNC machines would not be possible without CAD systems. The Geodesic Dome (Richard Buckminster Fuller, 1954), the undulating roof at Kansai airport (Renzo Piano, 1988–1994) and the International Terminal at Waterloo Station (7) in London (Nicolas Grimshaw, 1990–1994) were seminal projects. Greg Lynn studied the animation of forms using computer-generated models with his Embryological House in 1999. In this case, a complex organic 3D grid system was created with CAD systems.

Finally, vernacular architecture, a term which conjures images of classical or traditional architecture, can have different stylistic consequences in the context of systems. If vernacular architecture is understood as the architecture intrinsic to a place and to its function, it can certainly be modified to meet today's building standards of a house in an industrialised, digitalised place for a changing nuclear family. The modified vernacular architecture, as demonstrated in Vorarlberg, in the western part of Austria, is a perfect example of this. Modern buildings are adapted to the needs of the modern family and the requirement of energy efficiency, while still using local materials. The compact and simple forms of the architecture are suitable for smaller families but blend into the traditional context of a community previously characterised by agriculture (8).

Objectives

The objectives of this book are twofold: the main objective is to present to the young practitioner the current status of prefabricated building by documenting the different systems according to building typology and building components, thus systematically weaving a picture of the world of prefabricated systems. The documentation is supplemented with photos and drawings setting a clear framework of creative processes. The second objective is to discuss the following questions: do the architect's aims of achiev-

7

International Terminal, Waterloo Station, London, Nicholas Grimshaw & Partners, 1993

The 400 m long roof is made up of standard-sized glass sheets, which overlap and use a concertina joint to accommodate the double curve of the roof section and the track path.

ing individuality and artistic expression suffer from the modularising, codifying and repetition associated with prefabricated or preassembled building systems? Or does the architect gain flexibility in design as the building systems offer a high standard of quality?

Book organisation

Following this introduction, the chapter on the history of building systems highlights a few exemplary moments in the long story of building systems. The included prefabricated systems are not necessarily the most successful or ideologically the best examples of system building. The failures and visions were as important as the commercial successes.

The chapters on housing and commercial or industrial buildings document examples that delineate certain aspects, such as the different building construction methods. The chapter on housing covers the basic construction types, the extent of prefabrication and its implications on site and the issue of cultures, façades and their "cross-referencing" of styles. Commercial, or non-residential buildings, make up most of the built prefabricated architecture. The building type is broken down into three categories: temporary buildings, serial buildings and individual buildings. Modular concepts, flexibility, and construction methods are addressed here.

The fifth chapter, on the procedure of manufacturing a building, covers aspects concerning the logistics of planning, production, transportation and the assembly of a building. The efficiency of the manufacturers, their productivity, adaptability to different needs and standards are networked aspects of the building procedure. The aim is not to collect the latest tips on production or operation and materials of the market, but to dissect, display and analyse the matrix of methods and materials.

The chapter on components classifies the building's tectonics – systems, subsystems – and takes into account the developer's point of view; each layer is a clear building part allocated to a contractor, such as the loadbearing structure or building services. The final chapter opens a perspective on the future of prefabricated architecture.

We, the authors, hope to deliver a straightforward and informative collection of facts on building systems and at the same time offer insight into typically non-tectonic issues that form the systems in the first place.

8

Houses in Vorarlberg, Austria
The modern form of industrialised architecture is a gradual shift away from the vernacular.

9

Design exhibition Entry 06, Essen, Germany, 2006
Computer-generated organic forms bring a new dimension into the field of prefabricated architecture.

2 | History of Building Systems

What is the essential target of building systems? The systemisation of any building technology aims at producing more efficient and more cost-effective buildings than traditional methods. Systems of building and the subsequent variety of architectural "Gestalt" took their cues from the cultures of peoples, the geography and its natural resources, technological advances and, especially, the visions of architects and engineers. Thus, pinpointing the beginnings of building systems is quite challenging. Although developments in industrialisation, transportation and communication have internationalised the building industry to some extent, significant differences remain between countries and their attitudes toward building systems.

This chapter traces the history of building systems and its path of advancements in different contexts. The mobility, flexibility, security and economy achieved by various building systems are crucial to present-day better living and working conditions. At some moments in history, however, building systems offered the quickest, barely adequate shelters as a matter of survival. The examples shown in this chapter illustrate that the development of building systems did not only depend on the successes – some were expensive failures that were nevertheless important in the pursuit of architectural qualities and aspirations.

Early systems

The Mongolian yurt

For over 2,000 years, nomadic tribes have been travelling in the steppe regions of Mongolia with their families and homes in the cyclic search for pastures to resource food and trade crafts. The yurts, the traditional homes of the Mongolians, are light, transportable and easily built (1). Made of pliable wooden worm fences, woollen blankets, ropes made of yak- and horsehair and linen sheets, the yurts, also called gers, are raised and dismantled within 60 minutes and can be transported by two or three camels. The round form provides the maximum area for the given material, and the aerodynamic roof shape fends off the winds. The woollen blankets provide thermal insulation against temperatures that can reach −40 °C and the outer layer of linen provides protection against rain (2). The weight and size limitations of transportation by camel are clear practical criteria for the building system of yurts.

1

Mongolian yurt
The Mongolian yurts are conveniently compact for transport on camels yet provide secure shelter and display traditional values. The nomads recamp two to four times a year, so the efficient use of the steppe region resources is a necessity.

2

Silk painting "The Birth of the Child", Ming Dynasty, China, early 15th century
This painting from *The Story of Lady Wen-Chi* depicts a Mongolian royal encampment in the desert. Geometrically arranged linen sheet panels extend the noble court space around the yurt and separate it from the servants' area. In this example of nomadic architecture, the structure, though temporary, is a place of high stature.

The tatami mat in Japan

The Japanese tatami mat flooring element is the revised standard module of common architectural measure that has been used in Asia for over 1,000 years. The tatami mats, with measurements of 6 shaku 3 sun (190 cm) by 3 shaku 1.5 sun (95 cm), are the basis upon which the spacing and sizes of the columns, sliding doors, verandas and eaves are still determined today. Slight variations in size apply to different regions in Japan, but this system of building with elements as measurement modules has allowed the development of a remarkably high standard of craftsmanship and the standardisation of highly refined technical and functional details.

It is important to note here that the term "module" in architecture refers to a standard unit of measure used to determine the size of building components. The tatami is an example (3–5), as is the shaku (30.3 cm), the 1.25 m module in Germany or the 2 × 4 inch (5.1 × 10.2 cm) module in the USA. Many modules and variations exist, the most well-known ones being those developed by architects Leonardo da Vinci and Le Corbusier. This is not to be confused with the contemporary use of the term "module" referring to fully fitted-out boxes, sometimes interlocking, which are produced as finished products for living or working in.

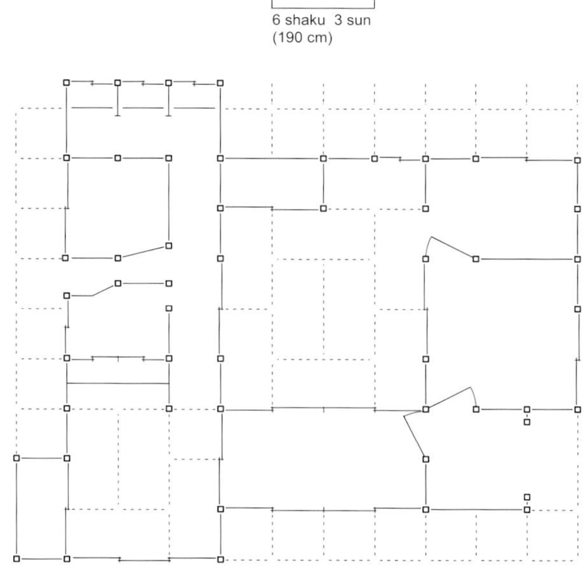

3

Japanese house
The organisation of a typical Japanese home uses the tatami mat module.

4

Tatami house
This illustration from the 18th century shows modular components set within a skeletal construction. Sliding wall elements allow a flexible open plan.

5

Tatami room
In Japan, room size is still measured in tatamis. For example, a four and a half tatami room is roughly 9 m^2.

Industrial Revolution and Machine Age

The Industrial Revolution spanned from the late 18th century to the 1840s and is responsible for a shift in technical, socioeconomic and cultural conditions that continues to reverberate in many aspects of our daily lives today, including our built surroundings. It is the era in which machinery replaced manpower. The textile and metallurgy industries soared and the steam engine was a milestone in the history of manufacturing. The Second Industrial Revolution began around the 1850s and saw the prowess of the new industrial giants Germany and the USA, who profited from "borrowing" ideas from Great Britain and still had capital to invest. Transportation in the USA expanded to vast, new dimensions with faster and better shipbuilding, and the railway industry, continually in higher demand, doubled its output 14 times since the first mass-produced steel tracks were laid. Food, drink, glass, soap, paper and textile industries profited from the improved availability of sodium carbonate and sulphuric acid. Longer working hours but also safer streets were possible thanks to gas, and later, electric lighting. New modes of communication and entertainment such as the telephone, phonograph, radio and cinema had an enormous impact on the social and cultural manifestations as analysed by the historian of popular culture Marshall McLuhan in his book *Understanding Media* (1964). The automobile industry redefined the concept of mobility and was essential to the development of materials and manufacturing procedures (6).

In the context of the Industrial Age, Reyner Banham, the inventor of modern architectural terms and a proponent of machine aesthetics, clarified the position and tendencies of an evolving era of architecture and design. In 1960, 180 years into the Industrial Age, he wrote one of the most influential critical books on architecture and design: *Theory and Design in the First Machine Age*. In it he coined the term "First Machine Age", which covers the early 20th century, as the age defined by electricity and light, various domestic electrical appliances, the portable typing machine and the automobile. Factory-made products gave way to a "machine aesthetic" that was driven by Walter Gropius as the leader of the progressive Bauhaus in 1923, and exemplified by the practicality and functional reduction of design and architecture.

6

Volkswagen factory
The perfection of the assembly line and mass production in the automobile industry was an invention of a system of manufacturing that was inspirational to the building of the home.

Mass production: from automobiles to architecture

Henry Ford's proclamation in 1908, "I will build a car for the great multitude", has long since been realised. Ford's dream of creating an automobile that the average American could afford was achieved by rationalising the production through the introduction of the assembly line and investing in new techniques and materials, resulting in higher efficiency and lower costs. And, the commodity of industrialised products, including buildings, was a solid platform for design.

7

Single family home and semi-detached house, Weißenhofsiedlung Stuttgart, Le Corbusier, 1927
The industrial production of the structure and components of the home, along with its reduced form, was a move away from traditionalist thinking.

The automobile was an object of fascination for Le Corbusier, undoubtedly the most influential architect of the Modern Movement. The Swiss architect, planner and visionary said in his manifest, *Toward an Architecture* (1922), that "The house is a machine for living in" (Le Corbusier, *Toward an Architecture*, Los Angeles, Getty Research Institute, 2007, p. 151). The Maison Citrohan, first designed in 1920, carries the name of the brand Citroën as a direct reference to the automobile. In other words, the house is like an automobile, its design engineered and reduced to suit its function.

Le Corbusier refers to the dream of the mass production of a house type. He imagined that components of houses, like automobiles, should be built in factories, a visionary idea to pronounce at that time but not illogical considering the power of industrialisation (7). The two aspects – the modern style of Functionalism and mass production of buildings – have since then been associated with one another and received with both positive and negative reverberations from the public.

The Maison Citrohan is only one of many prototypes, ideas and plans that were new and exciting among architects, but the idea of prefabricated homes did not take off immediately due to the unsettling effect this change in the feeling of "home" had for the inhabitants. Modernity and mass production in architecture continued to be met with opposition from conservatives who valued identity, tradition, crafts and the professionalism of the architect – traits that were thought to disappear with serial building. This negative association deterred the industrialisation of architecture; this was still the case in 1960, at the time of Banham's writing. The Second Machine Age, a term coined by fellow architectural critic Martin Pawley, was at its peak: luxury products were mass-produced (8), meaning that such an abundance and choice allowed the middle class to afford the luxuries individually. A new awareness of machine aesthetics as a conscious stylisation of electric gadgets, automobiles, furniture and architecture – as apparent in Italian industrial design (9), and Eames's chairs and homes – grew, but the industrialisation of architecture did not.

8

Braun Sixtant SM2 electric shaver, Gerd Alfred Müller and Hans Gugelot, 1961
This model, one of the many products that epitomised German modern industrial design, became a global player in electric shaving.

9

Valentine typewriter, Olivetti, Ettore Sottsass, 1969
The stylised typewriter replaced bulky cast-iron ones and was more affordable because it was mass-produced.

Milestones in building systems

American Dream and housing boom

The USA experienced a housing boom in the 1920s and 1930s, and fast-track, balloon-framed mail-order catalogue houses were sold by the thousands. Wood was plentiful, and the building industry in the USA grew rapidly after saw-cut timber and mass-produced nails came to existence (10). Until this point in time balloon housing was traditionally made, but with mail-order catalogue houses, they were industrialised, standardised and systemised (11). The "Ready Cut" posts, the flooring, wood siding, sheathing and interior fittings were included in the package. Kit houses by companies like Aladdin Homes and Sears, Roebuck and Co. boomed mainly in the Northeast and the Midwest, where the railroads were newly laid. Interestingly, the houses borrowed styles and carried labels like the California Bungalow, The Spanish Eclectic, The Victorian and the Cape Cod Cottage (13) and were decisively traditional. They resembled the conventional light-frame or brick alternatives, but were built in record time, cheaper (Sears claimed prefabrication saved 40 % in labour costs) and were of a better quality (12). The system behind the "Ready Cut" succeeded.

Besides the fast-track growth of wood housing, the USA was experiencing a new system of building with another material: cast iron. The malleability of iron façades easily took on the intricate forms of classical façades, so that "traditional" looking façades could quickly be applied. European countries had already developed its use (14), but the inventor James Bogardus of New York City was one of the first to mass-produce cast-iron beams, columns and façades that replaced massive structures and materials like stone and brick. As in the housing sector, Bogardus's cast-iron architecture spread across the USA and embraced the styles originating from Europe.

Progress in Europe

In Europe, prefabricated architecture was developing its own modern architectural language as we saw in the example of the Maison Citrohan, but on the commercial level the idea of building systems experienced a number of false starts. Modern European architecture was given a major impetus through the work of Walter Gropius and the founding of the Bauhaus, the most influential school of art and architecture in the 20th century, in 1919. Closely tied with various sectors like household products, painting and plastic arts, architects experimented with new architectural forms for industrial production. Prefabrication in architecture was not new: wooden military barracks, corrugated metal churches in the colonies and factories built of factory-made cast iron were already familiar images.

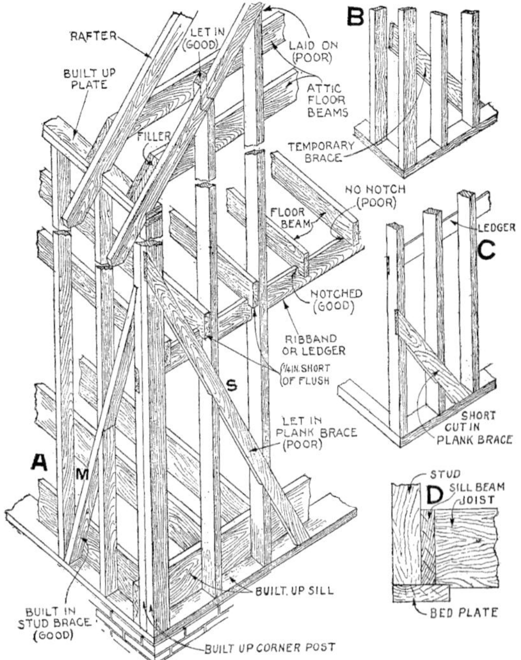

10

Balloon frame
The 2 × 4 inch (5.1 × 10.2 cm) wood frame construction was revolutionised by the invention of the steam engine, which enabled the production of steel nails and the saw cutting of wood.

11

Levittown, Pennsylvania, 1959
Fast-track, balloon-framed houses were planned and developed as a complete suburban community.

12

Modern Homes catalogue, 1920
The cover of the Sears, Roebuck and Co. catalogue featuring homes that could be ordered and delivered within weeks.

German developments

The pilot project Berlin-Friedrichsfelde in 1924–1926 by Martin Wagner, the head of the German Housing Provision (DEWOG), was a pre-war experiment in concrete slab construction (15). Housing shortages caused by the First World War had necessitated an alternative method of building that could replace the slower bricklaying methods of the time. The modified "System Occident" was adapted from the shuttering and erection techniques of the double-storey concrete slabs by the American engineer Grosvenor Atterbury. The 11 × 4 m slabs were only 25 cm thick. The use of cranes to lift the large slabs proved difficult and uneconomical, and the pre-planned designs did not accommodate the large inaccuracies that occurred during the drying process.

Ernst May, the city planning advisor of Frankfurt, also looked to Atterbury's assembly methods and devised the "Frankfurter

14

Cast-iron roof structure from the 19th century in a train station in Detmold, Germany
Cast iron was used in factories, railroads and other building types where larger spans were required. This became quickly popular in both Europe and the USA.

13

Modern Homes catalogue, 1934
This Sears, Roebuck and Co. catalogue kept an eye on the styles originating from Europe.

Plattenbau" (Frankfurt Slab System). The slabs were smaller, with maximum dimensions of 300 × 110 × 20 cm, handled with smaller rotating tower cranes and, most importantly, manufactured off-site in the factory. The construction time was significantly reduced compared to conventional building and until 1930, the "Frankfurter Plattenbau" was the foremost construction technique in town with 1,000 houses accredited to this method. However, the financial advantages were minimal and the houses suffered technical problems such as cracks and chips in the concrete and high levels of humidity. Unfortunately, before these problems could be resolved, other critical, psychological aspects like the sterile environment of the home through heavy standardisation and reservations about the coldness of the still unfamiliar concrete drew heavy criticism. This was worsened by the aversion toward Functionalism (from, of all people, the right-winged German Nationalists and the National Socialists) and the loss of jobs caused by rationalised building methods that were actually a response to the lack of skilled labour. The banks stopped financing the projects, May left the city, and the city-owned factories that had built them eventually closed down.

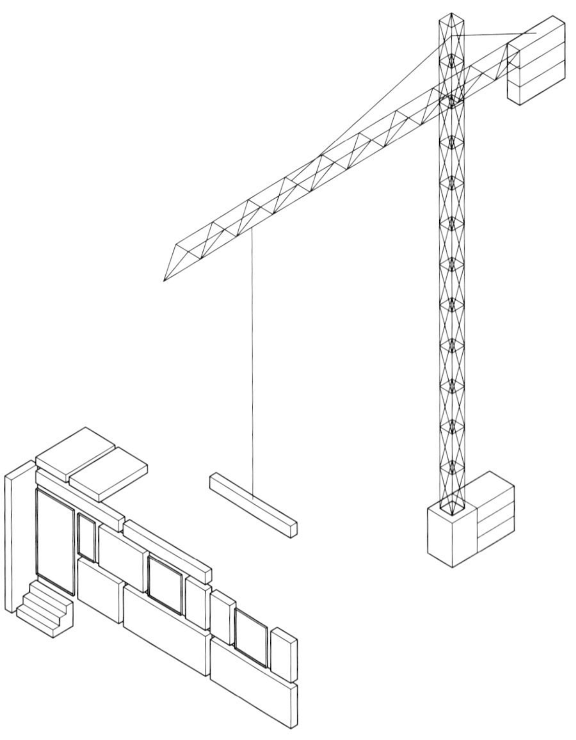

16

Assembly system of "Frankfurter Plattenbau", Ernst May, 1926–1930

The Frankfurt Slab System by Ernst May in 1926–1930 used smaller slabs than the System Occident, that were factory-made and assembled with smaller and easily manoeuvrable cranes.

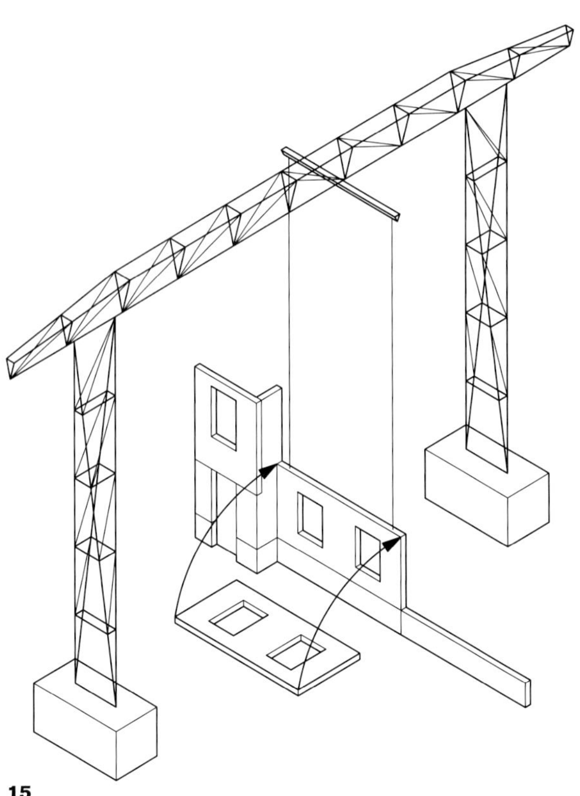

15

Concrete slab construction "System Occident", Berlin-Friedrichsfelde, Martin Wagner, 1924–1926

System Occident was a large concrete slab construction modelled after American prototypes. The slabs were "prefabricated" on site. Despite technical problems, this method was an important precedent for future slab systems.

17

"Frankfurter Plattenbau", Ernst May, 1926–1930, under construction

A factory-manufactured house of this type was one of the few concrete structures to be presented at the Weißenhofsiedlung in Stuttgart in 1927.

The "Frankfurter Küche" was the first mass-produced kitchen and a revolutionary experiment in the rationalisation of domestic work, and is still of relevance to kitchen planning today. Built within the framework of Ernst May's Frankfurt housing projects (16, 17) by the Viennese architect Margarete Schütte-Lihotzky, the kitchen design was based on analyses of the woman's kitchen work (18). All elements were optimised to reduce redundant movements and save space within the small kitchen size of 1.87 × 3.44 m. Kitchens for 15,000 flats were produced for the price of 238.50 German Reichsmark each from 1926–1930.

Eventually, standardised unit dimensions allowed parts to be mixed and interchanged at will (19), functioning along the same principles with which the assembly line worked in the production of automobiles. Even today, the 60 cm kitchen module offers the customer choice and the manufacturer the security of "fitting in". The globalisation of the kitchen as a coordinated set of modules is reminiscent of modularisation in the building industry with guidelines such as the Building Research Station Module Chart of 1960 (34), issued by the BRS (later succeeded by the Building Research Establishment, BRE), at that time a British government establishment charged with research, consultancy and testing for the construction sector.

18

Frankfurt Kitchen, Margarete Schütte-Lihotzky, 1926
The mass-produced kitchens were rationalised to save time and energy.

19

A box full of small-scaled kitchen components, around 1962
Customers could experiment with this model kitchen by the Dutch firm Bruynzeel. The kitchen components were held in place with magnets. Bruynzeel mass-produced efficiently planned built-in kitchen units for housing associations, architects and the government.

20

Dessau-Törten housing system, Germany, Walter Gropius, 1926–1928
This version with loadbearing walls and hollow-core slag-concrete blocks was produced on site within an optimised process for production and assembly.

From 1926 to 1928 Walter Gropius built 316 houses for low-income families in the Dessau-Törten suburban estate with his "honeycomb" construction method (20). This was originally developed at the Bauhaus as a modular system of standardised shuttering clustered in groups of four to twelve units and then poured with concrete. This proved impractical, and he opted for a simpler version with loadbearing walls of inexpensive prefabricated hollow-core slag-concrete blocks and ceilings of reinforced concrete beams. All materials were produced on site, but production and assembly were optimally rationalised with the assembly line, and sustainability and quality were controlled. Houses of 57–74 m^2 were being built at a rate of one per five and a half hours for the building structure, including the on-site casting of the blocks. Despite all these advancements, this project had to fail, following resurfacing resentment against the harsh forms and the technocratic appearance of the architecture. It seemed that these experiments with concrete were praised only by fellow architects.

The exhibition "Die Wohnung" (21), initiated by the Deutsche Werkbund in Stuttgart in 1927, was the climax of the modern era and featured the Weißenhofsiedlung, a suburban estate. It presented model houses for the modern urbanite, designed by 17 architects of the Modern Movement including Ludwig Mies van der Rohe (who designed the master plan), Walter Gropius, Le Corbusier, Bruno Taut, Jacobus Johannes Pieter Oud and Peter Behrens. In addition to proposing a new way of living with pure forms, optimal light and a minimum of clutter, the goal was to demonstrate the achievement of new materials and methods of construction, form-givers of the "New Architecture". A number of the houses were constructed with variations of Ernst May's

21

Poster for the exhibition of the Deutsche Werkbund, "Die Wohnung", Willi Baumeister, 1927

The posters for the exhibition clearly express the disapproval of clutter and ornament in living spaces.

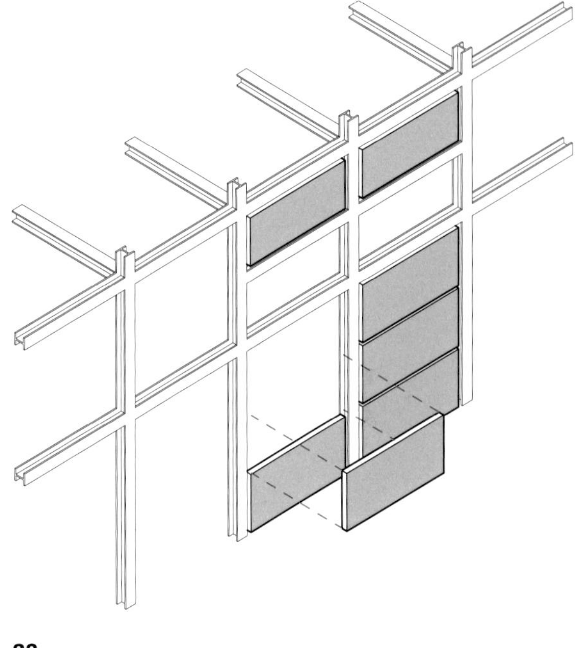

22

House No. 17, Weißenhofsiedlung Stuttgart, Walter Gropius, 1927

Gropius's house was a steel-framed structure with prefabricated light infill panels. Such new methods of construction suited the new, pure way of living proposed at the housing show.

concrete slab, but the majority of the houses were steel frames with prefabricated lightweight panels (22, 23). Other materials, such as the hollow-core slag (pumice-concrete blocks), zig-zag wood panels (as made by Feifel near Stuttgart) and thermal slabs, were also used. As many parts were produced in the factory, the 63 apartments in the 21 houses were constructed within 21 weeks. Visitor attendance was high, but, as usual, the concept of change in ideology of art and architecture was met with opposition from the public, even before the opening.

23

Multi-family housing, Weißenhofsiedlung Stuttgart, Ludwig Mies van der Rohe, 1927
The steel-framed structure of Mies van der Rohe's apartment block allowed freedom of the division of spaces inside.

24

Le Haut du Lièvre, Nancy, France, Bernard Zehrfuss, 1960
The housing block Le Haut du Lièvre was built with the Estiot system, using prefabricated reinforced concrete.

Slab building and social housing

The lessons learned before the war, especially with concrete, were reapplied in the early 1960s with social housing programmes. Large concrete panel systems accounted for 60 % of all housing in the German Democratic Republic in 1970, 50 % of all housing in Finland in the 1980s and a remarkable 75 % of all housing in the Soviet Union by the 1990s (27, 28). Eventually, the skeletal frame with concrete infill panels took form, and practically all buildings integrated at least prefabricated stairs, balconies and building services.

The "Plattenbau" (literally slab building) was the response to the post-war housing shortage and dominated the residential landscape of the German Democratic Republic. Initiatives to improve ecological or design aspects were ignored. In Leipzig, cost savings were achieved by using only 13 out of 39 possible components, but this led inevitably to monotony. The negative image of concrete has taken a turn since 1989, when "Plattenbau" projects were reinterpreted, demonstrating the advantages of this building method. For one, building components could be demounted and reused, but also built projects could be refurbished to suit other living and communal arrangements. In this manner, the architect Stefan Forster transformed a 180 m long large slab building into eight four-storey town villas by removing a floor level and seven vertical segments (25). Today, the "Plattenbau" is the centre of much debate, focusing on critical topics such as the overall organisation of housing developments and the outward appearance.

The Corviale (26), the 1 km long 1970s imitation of Le Corbusier's Unité d'Habitation on the periphery of Rome for 8,000 residents, did not live up to its intention as a heroic architectural monument nor as a housing solution. It was awesomely ambitious, but like other similar projects of this scale (24), became subjected to vandalism and ghetto-like conditions. The housing block of Pruitt Igoe in the USA was dramatically demolished in 1972 because of its social and structural deficiencies and is seen today as a typical example of this building type spinning out of control.

25

Leinefelde town villas, Germany, Stefan Forster Architekten, 2001–2004
A GDR slab building from the 1970s was the point of departure for a refurbishment project. The architect Stefan Forster transformed the 180 m long building into eight four-storey town villas by removing a floor level and seven vertical segments.

26

La Corviale housing project, Rome, 1972–1974
The prefabricated concrete La Corviale housing block by architects M. Fiorentino, F. Gorio, P. M. Lugli, G. Sterbini, M. Valori and others is well known for its monumentality and its failure as a social concept. Because the housing complex is a cultural monument to the 1970s, there are new initiatives to save the project.

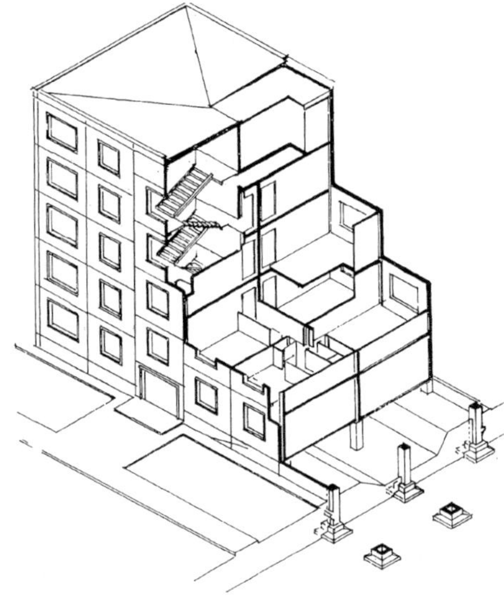

27

Overview Russian large-panel prefab system
Storey-high large panels were the predominant method of prefabrication in the Soviet Union, where the majority of homes were prefabricated.

British developments

An early example of industrialised system building construction was the Crystal Palace, designed by the gardener Joseph Paxton in 1851 for the Great Exhibition in London (29–31). At a time when buildings were made of stone and took many years to erect, the Crystal Palace was designed, manufactured and assembled in eight months. This was only possible through the manufacturing of a kit of parts in the factory and the ingenious idea of using repetitive, self-supporting bays that could be erected independent from one another by unskilled workers. Columns were composite structures that could be connected to extensions or various decorative features, all glass panels were of standard dimensions and the supporting framework was dimensioned accordingly. The exhibition hall was a complete building system of modules, components and connections. It also employed system integration encompassing drainage, operable ventilation and natural light. Its significance lies not in its large volume nor in the pioneering modular iron prefabricated structure, but in its reliance upon and extension of the rationalisation process to the entire construction site, from factory to site.

Industrialised building was already flourishing before the First World War in Great Britain whose industry was manufacturing, packaging and shipping homes, churches, storage houses and just about every necessary structure for colonies in Asia and

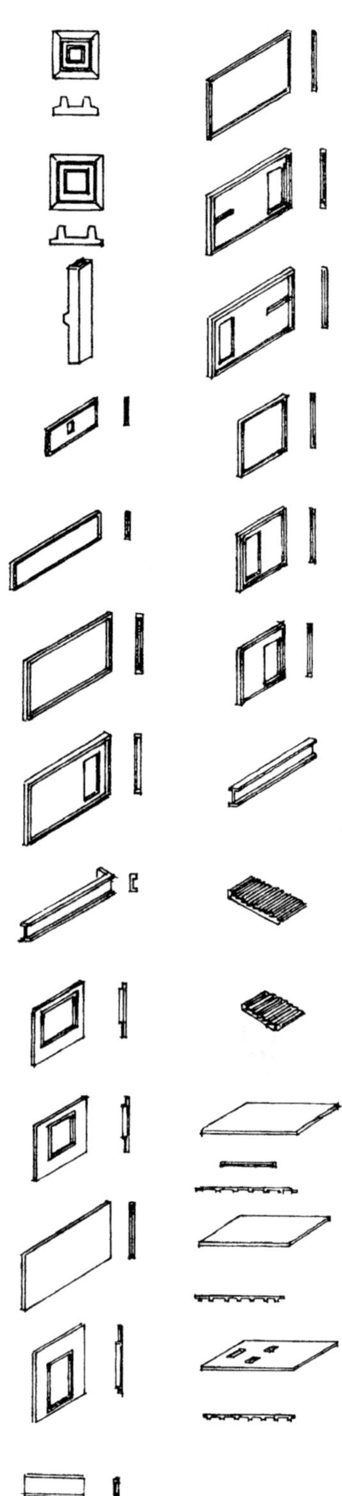

28

Elements of a Russian large-panel prefab system
System building requires a minimal number of elements used to economise building costs, but should optimally differentiate the outer forms and allow varying floor arrangements.

Africa. Even earlier, there was great demand from the Wild West frontier leading up to California as construction companies during the gold rush in 1848–1855 could hardly meet the need for quick dwellings. Portable cottages made of wood or iron were sent in large numbers by ship. Corrugated iron, useful for its lightness and durability, was also popular; however, in subtropical regions the material proved to be lacking in thermal mass. Ingenious technical advances in the material qualities and production of the heavier, more substantial material cast iron as partial or total building systems were made, especially in England and Scotland. The longer spans of the main structure allowed for large non-obstructed spaces, useful in factories with large machines.

29

Crystal Palace, London, Joseph Paxton, 1851
Designed by the gardener Joseph Paxton for the London Great Exhibition, it is a paradigm example of industrialised system building. All modules, components and connections were manufactured in the factory.

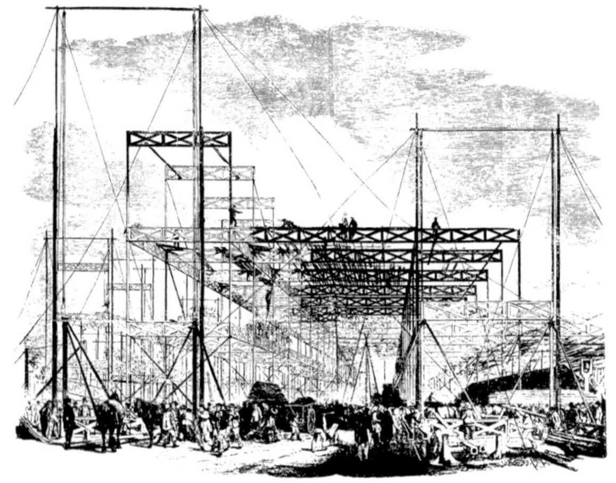

30

Crystal Palace modules
All components down to the window mullions and sashes were engineered to integrate natural ventilation, lighting and drainage.

1 Alternative (pre-industrial) proposals for the Crystal Palace involved traditional materials and methods that would have required a building time of three years.

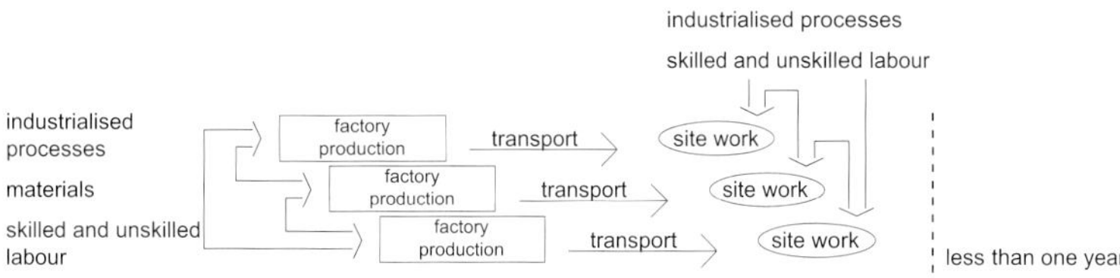

2 J. Paxton's design was also an organisational concept. The flow of materials, production of systems and subsystems, labour and assembly were organised as a planned sequence of events.

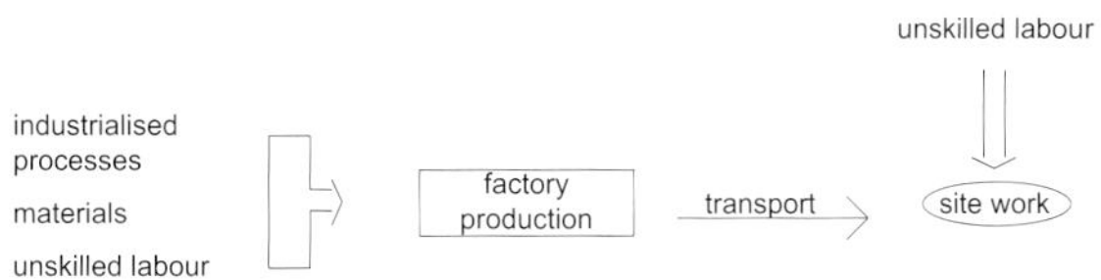

3 In the typical work flow of prefabricated houses, all components can be assembled by unskilled workers.

31

Crystal Palace systemisation
The highly sophisticated systemised rotation of labourers on and off site was key to the efficient production of the Crystal Palace. 500 m in length and 150 m wide, this extraordinary space was built by 2,000 men in six months.

Post-war prefabricated housing

After the First World War, Great Britain was one of the first states to subsidise social housing programmes. Since there was a shortage of skilled labour and traditional building materials, housing authorities looked to building systems as a way to build homes quickly and effectively. These alternative building techniques were to replace labour-intensive bricklaying, which accounted for 31 % of the cost, and carpentry, which accounted for a further 26 %. Many radical new systems (such as precast concrete frames or concrete blocks) were developed and built, but as in Germany, they were not as successful as anticipated, largely due to the lack of planning and development resulting partially from inconsistent government support. Technical problems such as cracking, leaking and corrosion occurred and in both countries the technical problems led to abandonment of the technology. The tarnished image of prefabrication persisted longer than the unresolved problems.

When the Second World War was over in 1945, the poor existing housing conditions, coupled with the lack of housing through war destruction, called for a new attempt with system housing, this time with a focus on temporary housing. The Ministry of Works in Great Britain initiated many projects, the first of these being the prefabricated bungalow, the Portal House of 1944, which was based on a lightweight steel frame. The extensive use of steel proved to be too costly so the Portal was never put into production, but became a precedent for many other experiments with different construction methods. These included the Arcon with steel-framed sections and asbestos sheets, the Uni-Seco with timber framing and asbestos cement-clad panels and the Tarran with a light timber frame construction and reinforced concrete panels. Mass production alleviated the housing shortage significantly: the Arcon group managed to produce a section in 12 minutes and produced 41,000 houses. Many of these ultimately outlived the predicted lifespan of 10–15 years, and even changed location as was the initial intention. The aluminium AIROH bungalow was a significant and curious landmark in mass production (32, 33). Built in a decommissioned aircraft factory, the building components consisted of four fully fitted sections of a house that were delivered by truck and bolted

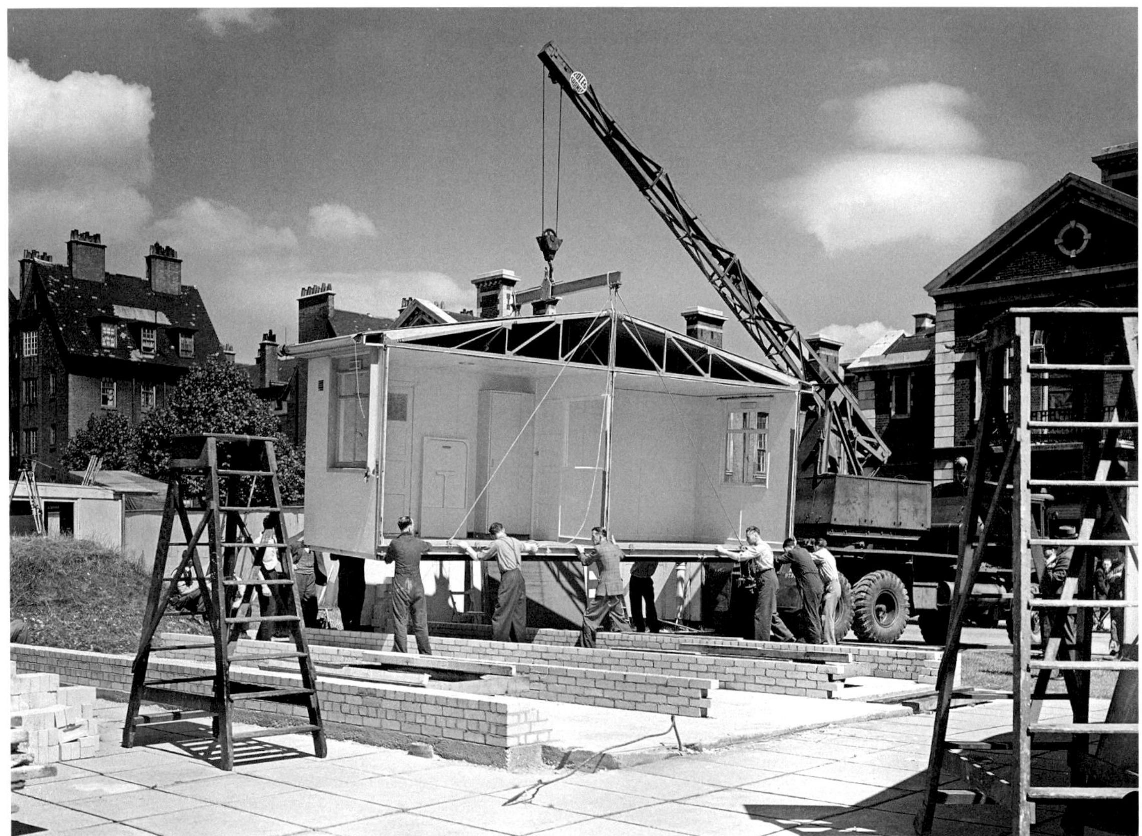

32

AIROH aluminium bungalows
The bungalows were complete with plumbing and wiring for standard kitchens.

together on site. The sections included bathrooms, refrigerators and plumbing not unlike the less technically advanced temporary houses for migrating dam builders, made by the Tennessee Valley Authority in the 1930s in the USA.

Small cladding units supported by independent structural frames still proved uneconomic and soon, in 1948, the Ministry found that, of the new systems, the large concrete panel was the cheapest. Still, since the Housing Act of 1944, the new methods of construction were able to account for 157,000 temporary houses built from 1945 to 1948, of which one third were AIROHs, but this number was significantly less than what had been expected.

When the responsibility for support of system housing shifted from the government to local authorities, it was the industrial cities that relied mostly on system building. Many of these were homes for higher densities, in particular, concrete high-rise buildings, later called tower blocks, like the "Plattenbau" of mainland Europe. The Wimpey No-Fines system was developed by the George Wimpey company and received much praise for its rationalised operation. It was based on a metal prefabricated framework and an in-situ concrete system, making it a combination prefab and on-site method. The system boasted 11 house types and was very successful. It comprised 27 building systems, the most popular of these being in-situ concrete systems, built 100,000 houses up to 1955 and experienced similar output well into the 1970s. This accounted for a third of all local authority housing!

The most important achievement of government research was the modular coordination in the 1960s (34), or the design of building to a common dimensional framework. This was fundamental to networking modular systems for prefabrication of interchangeable parts and would not have been developed by commercial firms alone. One of these applied a flexible low-rise system for housing to the steel frame system developed by CLASP, a local authority schools consortium that was responsible for a major school building programme.

The British large-panel concrete systems (such as Bison) were also developed to the modular system. These precast con-

33

AIROH aluminium bungalows installation process
The four sections were delivered by truck, positioned into place with a crane and bolted together.

34

Building Research Station Module Chart, 1960
This chart was established by the British BRS with standard opening sizes developed to facilitate mass production of building components. Modularised building components could be mixed and matched, and the building industry could focus on quality.

crete systems were mainly used for large housing projects of eight to 20 floors in height and integrated internal and external finishes, wiring and plumbing. The Larsen-Nielsen system from Denmark was adapted and was built by the hundreds in the London area.

Although the centralised modular system was a success for the production of many building types, system building declined due to changes in government policies. Technical problems were not to be overseen, and finally the 1967 economic crisis opened views that system building was too expensive and inadequate. Special attention was drawn by the 1968 collapse of the just finished 22-storey Ronan Point, built with the Larsen Nielsen large-panel system. An explosion on the 18th floor caused a progressive collapse of the entire southeast corner, allowing speculations that the building type was the cause. Though it was proven in 1970 that system building was indeed cheaper than traditional building for all house types and that the collapse was not at all related to the form of construction, system building was not to receive any further sponsoring. Traditional building methods were to take over again.

In the countries mentioned in this chapter, the more successful methods relied heavily on the traditional outward appearance applied to an inherently different concept of architecture while most of the building systems with "modern" forms suffered negative branding. There are, however, timeless documents from the past 60 years that embody the spirit of the time, express the new materials and technology and continue to inspire the development of architecture built with systems.

Case Study Houses

The Case Study Houses were brought to life by Los Angeles-based *Arts & Architecture* magazine and its publisher, John Entenza, between 1945 and 1966. The American public, like the British and German public, was showing little enthusiasm for new, "industrialised" forms in housing. Traditional appearances were the norm, and this was frustrating for architects who were discovering exciting potential in mass-produced housing. In California, where the boundary between inside and outside is climatically and culturally more open, a landscape of open architecture had developed. Architects like Irving Gill, Richard Neutra, Frank Lloyd Wright and Rudolph Schindler were closing the generation gap between traditional bungalow architecture and the Angeleno Modern. Hispanic influence can be seen in Gill's work, the International Style background in the Viennese Neutra and Schindler, and Japanese influence in Frank Lloyd Wright. John Entenza shared this openness, but he also had a sharp vision.

The goal of the Case Study programme was to promote a "good environment". Altogether, 36 prototypes for "mass production" were designed and built, but the generous layout made them only affordable by the financial elite, the progressive upper class. As in Stuttgart, the architects studied new techniques and honest, clear forms. The steel-framed houses were the most provocative and gave the progressive impulse of the programme, the most famous and rigorous of these being the CSH No. 8 by Charles and Ray Eames (35, 36). The exposed steel frame structure offers large expanses of unobstructed space with little structural mass while the façades are solid panels in various colours alternating with standard-sized glass panels that allow the light to filter in. Although the house is basically a steel and glass box, the furniture and exceptional handling of materials and form are what make it essentially a "home". The discovery of combining open spaces with living comfort inspired architects in Great Britain, Japan and all over the world to work with new methods.

The Case Study Houses were a major influence on the international modern architectural scene, specifically for the high-tech architecture of the 1980s. Many lessons from the Case

35

Case Study House No. 8, Charles and Ray Eames, Pacific Palisades, Los Angeles, 1945–1949
This steel and glass box embodies both new technologies and the comfort of the modern home. The façade expresses transparency, lightness and colour.

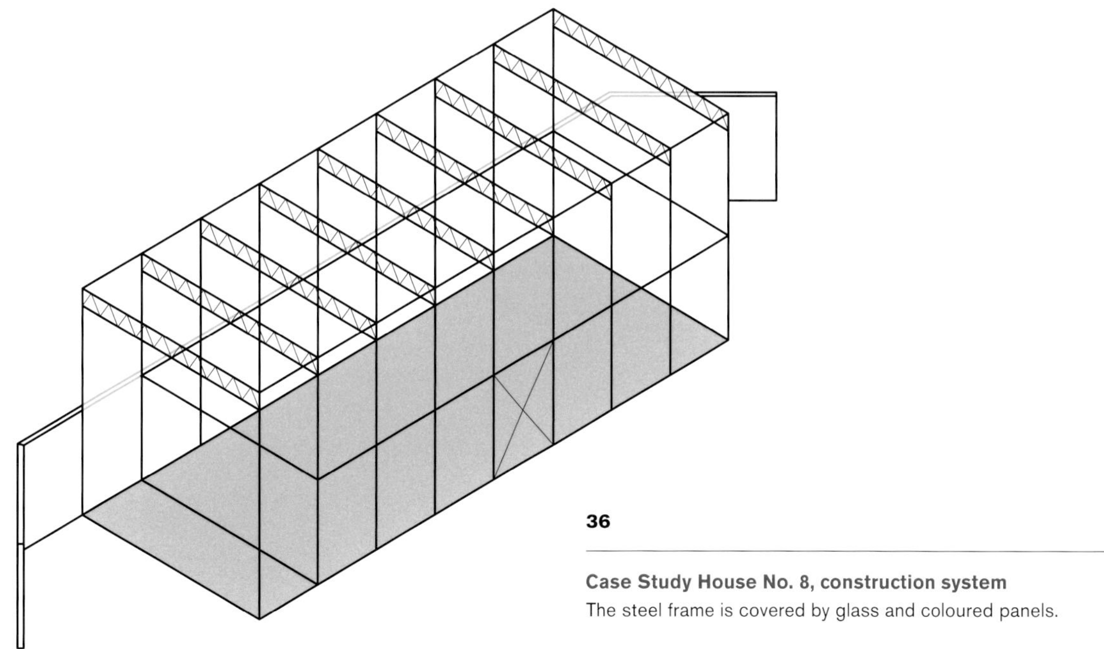

36

Case Study House No. 8, construction system
The steel frame is covered by glass and coloured panels.

Study Houses point back to Le Corbusier's "honest" approach to new materials like steel, glass and concrete. Still new to the world, was, for example, the idea that buildings made with steel or concrete columns no longer had loadbearing walls, and therefore permitted relatively open spaces. But the key issue was the industrialisation of building components, or at least the use of standardised components in a clearly new attitude toward the architecture of prefabrication (37).

The pioneers of prefab

The technological developments and newer manufacturing strategies in system building in the pre- and post-war years were not all in vain, even though they seemed to have enjoyed only intermittent success. It seems a long and weary process with many learning stages on the way, but it is also one abundant with thrills. As industrialisation played its hand in the building industry in USA, Germany, Great Britain, France and much of the industrialised world, several architects displayed monumental feats of architectural prowess while risking commercial failure.

37

Case Study House No. 22, Pierre Koenig, Los Angeles, 1959–1960
This L-shaped steel structure is one of the most radically reduced Case Study Houses. All elements were standard industrialised elements.

Jean Prouvé

If system building is at its most true, selective definition the prefabrication of components to be delivered, assembled to a complete (or variable) form and disassembled for further use, then the Maison Tropicale by Jean Prouvé is probably the first species of true system building in the 20th century. This prototype, one out of three ever built, was constructed in Prouvé's atelier in France, shipped by air cargo and then assembled in Brazzaville, Congo, in 1954. After some refurbishment, all three houses moved some half a century later to the banks of the Seine, the East River and the Thames.

Based on a 1 m modular system, the Maison Tropicale was designed as a prototype for inexpensive, readily assembled housing to be transported to French colonies in Africa (38–40). The house typology resembles that of Japanese architecture, albeit in metal and with round portholes, but is built to withstand hot temperatures and high levels of humidity. The sheet aluminium sliding doors, shaded terraces and originally raised floor level modulated air and light qualities in the relatively uniform space. Although so few were built, this project remains an important document of prefab culture.

38

Maison Tropicale, Jean Prouvé, 1954
A prefabricated house in the truest sense of the term, the project was first built in Congo. This one was dismantled some 50 years later and reassembled in New York.

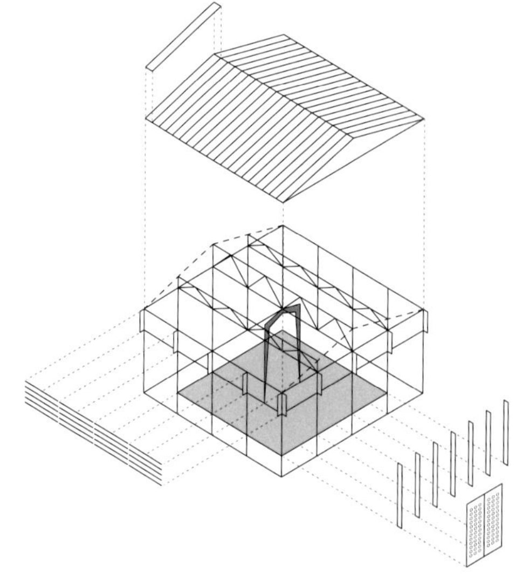

40

Maison Tropicale, Jean Prouvé, design 1949–1951
This house is made of components that would fill up two shipping containers today. All but the largest structural elements are aluminium. The heaviest piece weighed in at around 100 kg and could easily be handled by two men.

39

Maison Tropicale, Jean Prouvé, at the Tate Modern, London, presentation 2008
Its presentation in London demonstrates the house's ability to be dismantled, transported and reassembled.

Richard Buckminster Fuller

Buckminster Fuller was a navy seaman and a restless inventor with a fascination for geometry. At a time when most of America was purchasing prefabricated traditional homes, Fuller presented his first design of the futuristic looking Dymaxion House (1928). It was designed to be mass-produced: the body between two hexagonal compression rings was suspended from a mast which contained state-of-the-art electrical appliances (41). Aluminium, still a relatively unfamiliar material in the building industry at that time, was chosen for its lightness, high performance and durability. The round form allowed for a maximum of space in proportion to the material. The significant claim was that the house should weigh less than 3 tonnes – as little as a car, the icon of prefabrication. Unfortunately, with a fate similar to most other ambitious prefab projects, the idea could not establish itself in the building market and was never mass-produced due to the high price of aluminium.

Over a decade later, in 1940, the US military had several hundred 6 m wide military versions of the house, called DDU (for Dymaxion Deployment Unit), built and flown to the Pacific and Persian Gulf areas (42, 43). They were successful for the military, as the newer building method of adding from top to bottom cut crucial construction time. Compound curved panels improved the mast-hoisting process and withstood high winds, blasts and extreme weather conditions. Furthermore, the shadowless corners were easier to camouflage. The natural "chilling machine effect", whereby the heated air was sucked out of perimeter vents while cool air was pulled in from the top, was not

41

Dymaxion House, Richard Buckminster Fuller, 1928
This futuristic prototype was to have many derivatives to follow.

42

Dymaxion Deployment Unit, Buckminster Fuller
Hundreds of the military derivative of the Dymaxion House were constructed for the war in 1940. They were built top-down and had a natural ventilating effect.

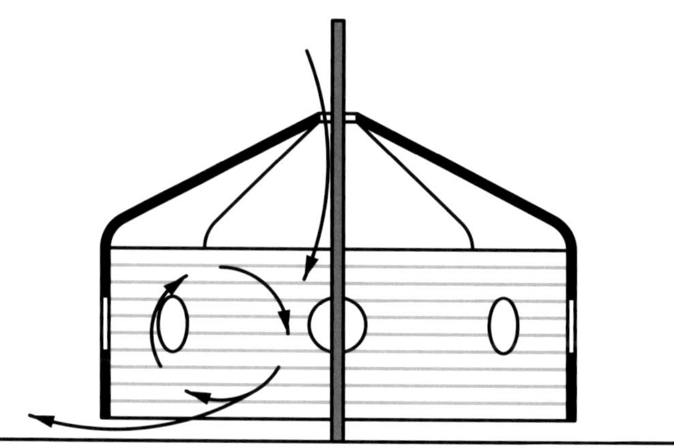

43

Diagram of Dymaxion Deployment Unit
The home version of the DDU was technically altered to achieve a natural ventilating effect that supposedly functioned despite contradictory physical principles.

used in the military DDU, but the technology was to be employed later in the Wichita House. It is interesting to note here the similarities between the DDU and the Mongolian yurt in terms of its exemplary building method and economy of form.

After the war came to an end in 1945, the Dymaxion would be technically advanced and meticulously modified to become the Dymaxion Dwelling Machine, also known as the Wichita House (44). Developed with a team of aircraft designers, engineers and craftsmen, the house was manufactured at Beech Aircraft factory in Wichita, Kansas. The 11 m wide dynamically formed houses were capable of being packed small and erected quickly, and were envisioned to be stackable and repeated to assume a neighbourhood atmosphere. The quality and performance was excellent. The interior fittings were of equal ingenuity: room-dividing storage-wall pods and the metal and plastic moulded Dymaxion bathroom allowed for ample and well-lit living spaces. The complete house weighed just under 3 tonnes – a normal house weighed 150 tonnes – and cost as much as a luxury automobile, just as predicted. After much marketing and public enthusiasm, the company received 3,500 orders. The architect, however, possibly for egotistical reasons, was not yet ready with revisions and claimed that the Dymaxion House needed seven more years of development time. The production, and all the visionary impetus that guided it, came to an end.

44

Wichita House, Wichita, Kansas, Richard Buckminster Fuller, 1945
The home version of the Dymaxion Deployment Unit was larger, modified with technically advanced interior fittings and still economically packed for easy transport.

Konrad Wachsmann

The collaboration of Konrad Wachsmann and Walter Gropius after their emigration to the USA lead to a utopian vision of a prefabricated house that merged pure forms and intricate detail. In 1942, the two presented a prototype for a modest but precisely built home of framework and panel construction. The Packaged House (45–47) was approved, generously funded by the government and well marketed, but the company sold no homes by the end of the war in 1945. Luckily, Wachsmann, this time without Gropius, had a second chance with a government-backed housing programme for veterans. Much more was invested in

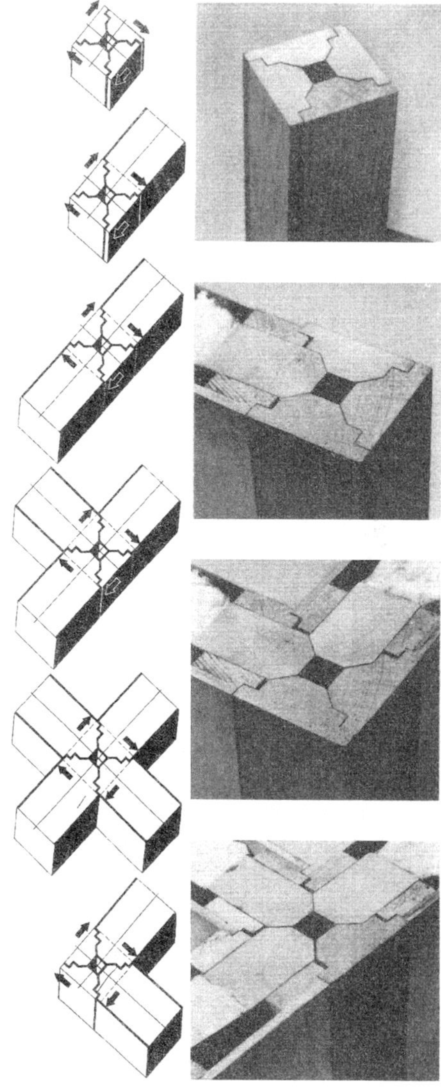

45

Connection detail of the Packaged House, Konrad Wachsmann, 1942
The construction principle of the inwardly focused connection elements allows a uniform outer surface.

new factory equipment and a change in management. Wachsmann, with experience in building with wood in Germany, redesigned and developed the system of panels and connections. Two years later, when production was ready, the government withdrew its funds and the production stopped. All in all, of the 10,000 houses that the General Panel Corporation expected to put out per year, 200 were produced and only a few were sold.

Fritz Haller

The Swiss architect and furniture maker Fritz Haller's holistic approach to building systems is a significant contribution to architecture. Haller masterminded the long-span Maxi (1963), the Mini (1969) and Midi (1980) systems (48), the well-known furniture system USM Haller and several utopian designs. In the first three systems, the building structure, building services and interior finishes were based on a geometric three-dimensional grid and fully integrated. This universality offered a high degree of variability, which in turn provided flexibility in the design of any building. The three building systems offer different degrees of complexity for different uses. The Midi building system, for example, the most complex of the three, comprises of a steel box system for building multi-storey highly mechanised buildings such as schools, laboratories and office buildings (49). The steel columns and double open-web trusses are fitted out with the Armilla installation model for all mechanical ducts, cable trays and fasteners.

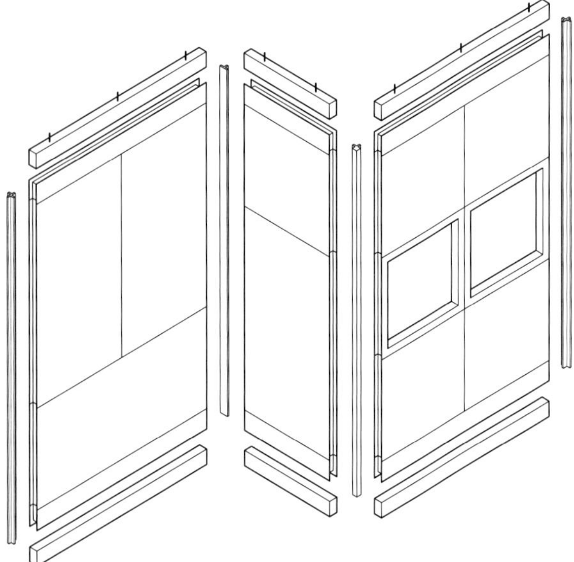

46

Construction principle of the Packaged House, Konrad Wachsmann, 1942
The system allows for a variety of layouts with the same detail principle.

47

Elevation of the Packaged House, Konrad Wachsmann, 1942
Only a few of the industrialised houses were sold, but the experience was a lesson on the technological, economic and social aspects of industrialised housing.

This highly sophisticated system never really took off. This has partly to do with the exclusivity of the total system that rejected interchangeability with other off-the-shelf products, leaving the potential buyer with a dependence on the system. The widely successful USM Haller office furniture systems are still produced today.

Alison and Peter Smithson

Alison and Peter Smithson of London were mainly known for their involvement with the movement of Team X and New Brutalism. With their House of the Future (50, 51), designed for the Ideal Home Exhibition in London in 1955–1956, an honest, direct approach to the new material plastic was consistent with the ideology of their previous works: the architecture was to suit the situation. Only 50 years young at that time, plastics were slowly introduced through industrial design products such as the telephone, records, furniture, automobile interiors and predictably made their way into the building sector. It was not for the first time that moulded organic forms were used in building. Buckminster Fuller invented metal bathrooms for the Dymaxion House, Paul Rudolph experimented with concrete. The House of the Future, complete with a private garden, was entirely formed in plastic-impregnated fibrous plaster. The curved forms substantially reduced cleaning time, in keeping with the changing role of the emancipated woman.

48

Midi system, Fritz Haller, 1980
The connection of a column and the double open-web roof trusses with a prefabricated steel construction.

50

House of the Future, Alison and Peter Smithson, 1955–1956, view from above
The house was constructed of plastic-impregnated fibre plasterboard.

49

Midi system in detail
View into the ceiling construction with the integrated mechanical services.

51

House of the Future, interior view
Built for the Ideal Home Exhibition in London, this house is prefabricated in parts and exemplifies the use of plastic as a low-maintenance material.

Paul Rudolph

Paul Rudolph is the American counterpart to the New Brutalism of Alison and Peter Smithson. As an architectural movement New Brutalism is defined not by stylistic terms, but is instead remembered for its fair-faced concrete and monolithic forms. The aesthetics of this architecture lie in its rationality and ordering system. The engine behind New Brutalism is the directness that drives the form and the movement: let the building show what it is about, express the mechanical systems and employ materials that work functionally.

52

The Oriental Masonic Gardens, New Haven, Connecticut, Paul Rudolph, 1968–1971
The buildings consist of clusters of modules within a double-storey pinwheel layout.

In 1968, Paul Rudolph designed the Oriental Masonic Gardens (52) for lower-income families in New Haven, Connecticut. Trailer-like boxes were trucked to the site and placed by cranes into double-storey pinwheel layouts delineating garden spaces. The prefab co-op is a systemised housing project on two levels: Rudolph takes on a social stance by adjusting to people's needs with groups of room-sized modular units clustered around a core for each home. The Oriental Masonic Gardens is also a spatial system, a pattern that contains sheltered spaces within the complex and has the ability to "spread out". It is a democratisation of modules and spaces with no hierarchy.

The Temple Street parking garage, also in New Haven, is not made of precast concrete systems, but defines abstract formalism in building systems (53). The building was designed to span a length of 265 m and to bridge a street, but this part was uncompleted. To break down the horizontality, the parapets are spliced at every double column and a vertical reading is possible from frontal angles. This is a system of rhythms used to group and regroup parts of a whole, like in music, in order to overlay scales of reading.

53

Temple Street Parking Garage, New Haven, Connecticut, Paul Rudolph, 1962
Typical of New Brutalism, the form is derived from the fluidity of the material.

3 | Systems in Housing

Building systems in housing represent a specific topic that merits a category of its own. Housing typology has undergone more experiments than any other building type and has the greatest variety of standards. After all, dwelling is a basic necessity and the living units are generally smaller, more plentiful and of a more temporary character than most other typologies. In short, every culture needs housing in large quantities, quickly and at a reasonable price – and this provides fertile ground for the development of systems. Thus, it is not surprising that many of the milestones in the history of building systems include examples of housing.

The attitude towards system building, or more specifically, prefabrication, has always been in a state of perpetual change. The quality and solidity of a house were associated by many with slow, more traditional building methods, which in turn substantiated its value. Le Corbusier stated in 1922 that "building one's house is a bit like making one's will" (Le Corbusier, *Toward an Architecture*, Los Angeles, Getty Research Institute, 2007, p. 262), a misconception that has repeatedly stalled the development of prefabrication of housing in countries such as Germany and Great Britain. On the other hand, prefabrication and other forms of system building use new materials, offering opportunities to improve an older system. In the Netherlands and the USA, technical progress and development of system building in the last half century have had positive resonance. In these countries, ownership is common, homes are more or less exchangeable, and they are a source of pride if they provide the space, the look, security and a technically adequate environment. Apartments, semi-detached houses, single-family houses and even student halls of residence and hotels to some extent fulfil the requirements of the home and contribute to endless possible combinations. For the sake of simplicity this chapter focuses mainly, but not exclusively, on the single-family home.

System building of the house can be categorised into the following basic construction types: light-frame construction, slab construction, modular and combined construction (1). The way building components are delivered influences the approach to and the extent of construction. The two seemingly opposite methods are on-site and prefab (factory-built). Flat-pack and modules are more complete types of packing and delivery.

Differences in culture explain the variety in aims, standards, styles and the role of system building have on the product called home. A look at the USA, Great Britain, the Netherlands, Austria and Japan provides an insight.

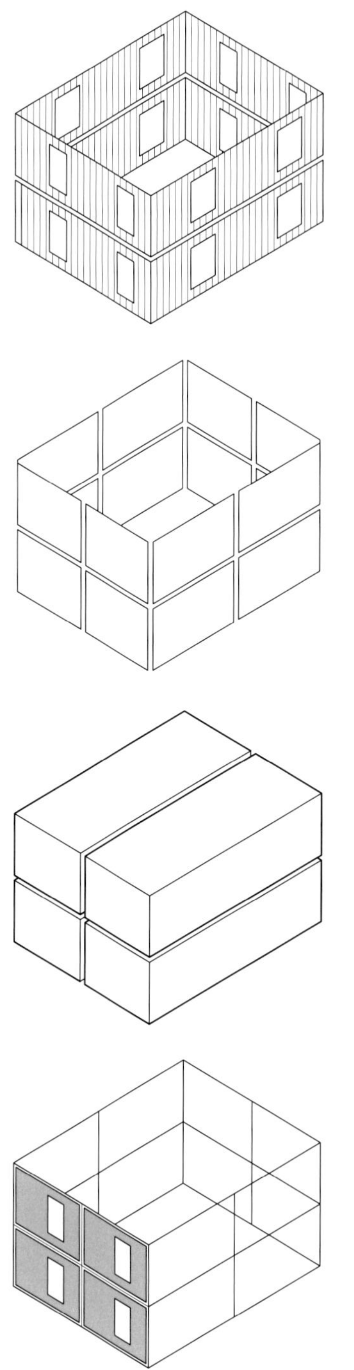

1

System building in housing
The basic construction types are: light-frame construction, slab construction, modular and combined construction.

Construction types

Light-frame construction

Light-frame construction is based on lightweight, linear structural members with a uniform cross section. The structural members, or studs, form a frame of exterior walls. Diagonal bracing members provided lateral stability in the past, but this arrangement has been superseded by carefully nailed rigid panels such as plywood sheathing, mineral fibreboard or engineered wood panels for higher shear strength. Cladding is added to the exterior to protect against weathering, and the voids between the studs are filled with soft insulation or rigid insulation boards attached to the studs. Two major light-frame building techniques used in the USA, Canada and the Scandinavian countries, where timber is plentiful, are the balloon frame and the platform frame (2), with the latter continuing to be the predominant method of construction in these countries today. These methods became especially popular after the invention of the industrially manufactured steel nail in the 19th century, which considerably alleviated the task of connecting wooden members.

The older balloon frame technique, which was common in the USA until the late 1940s, uses continuous vertical timber members, typically 2 × 4 inch (5.1 × 10.2 cm) or 2 × 6 inch (5.1 × 15.3 cm) placed at 16 inch (40.6 cm) centres. They extend from the base sill up to the top plate and support the intermediate floor joists and the roof rafters or trusses to a height of two storeys. The studs were lightweight and compact, making them easily transportable. Furthermore, the houses could be built without skilled labour. However, this system as a wooden structure has disadvantages, such as the requirement for long timber members and the tendency of wood to shrink over a period of time. Probably the greatest disadvantage of this technique is that the path of fire along the length of the members had to be obstructed with fire stops. This method of construction was consequently banned by certain building codes in the USA in the late 1940s. This building system has been largely replaced by platform framing, but today, since light-gauge steel construction has replaced the wood in the balloon frame, the older system has made a comeback.

The platform frame is similar to the balloon frame, with the exception that the wall frames (stud bays) are floor-height and the floor frames (joist bays) are built independently of one another (3–5). The platform frame can generally take up to four levels of walls and floors. For the roof construction, trusses are often preferred to wooden beams for their longer clear spans. Many standard configurations allow space for the installation of wiring, piping and ductwork. Roof trusses are often factory-built to reduce the requirement for site labour and to ensure dimensional stability and quality. Both light-frame structures, balloon and platform frame, are usually supported by a concrete slab foundation or foundation walls, which vary according to terrain and ground conditions.

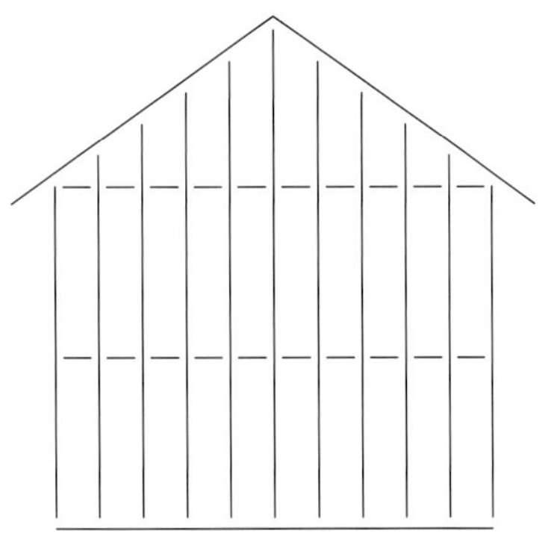

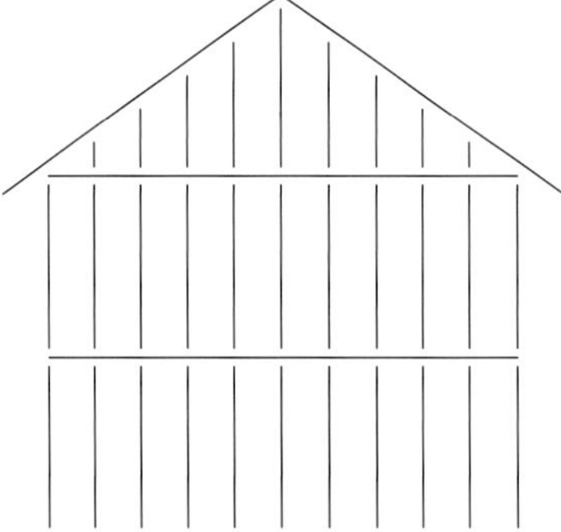

2

Balloon frame and platform frame

The diagrams of the light-frame construction types show parallel linear elements or studs. In the balloon frame, studs reach from the base sill past the intermediate floors up to the top plate. In the platform frame, the studs are connected from sole plates to top plates to form storey-high planar forms, or platforms.

3

Platform frame construction site: the skeletal structure
The structure is based on lightweight, uniform structural members assembled to form storey-high platforms.

4

Platform frame construction site: the envelope
The enclosure of the space provides stiffness to the structure.

5

Platform frame construction site: the finished building
The construction system is widely used in the USA and Scandinavian countries. Most of the assembly takes place on site and requires only unskilled labour.

Slab construction

Slab construction is based on planar structural members consisting of vertical loadbearing walls and horizontal slabs. As in a house of cards, each loadbearing wall is a structural unit able to support vertical loads from floor, wall and roof systems above. The walls must also resist lateral loads from supported floor and roof systems as well as wind loads, etc. Horizontal slabs must support dead (permanent loads from building structure) and live loads (moving and varying loads, such as occupants and furnishings).

Flooring systems of slab construction generally consist of precast concrete plank floor systems or in-situ reinforced concrete floor systems, depending on the required slab form and degree of prefabrication (6). Precasting structural elements allows for greater quality control of the concrete form and its structural integrity. If prestressed or post-tensioned, they have greater structural efficiency and can achieve longer spans. In comparison with other flooring systems, such as the conventional wood joist and plywood subfloor system, the floors in slab

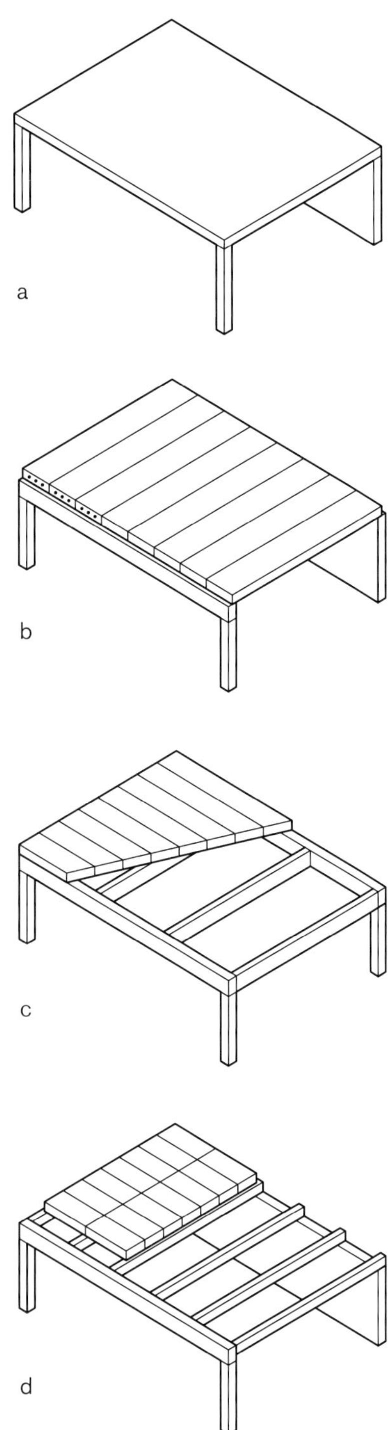

6

The degree of prefabrication in flooring is determined by time and cost constraints
The larger prefabricated concrete slab (a) requires less on-site time and has fewer connections, the prefabricated concrete plank floor (b) is less cumbersome during transportation and erection but is still structurally sound, while prefabricated concrete structural decking (c) and prefabricated panels (d) offer the most flexibility in planning.

7

Burger House, Detmold, Germany, raum 204, 2006
This house is built with large OSB boards, a product with fewer multifunctional attributes than the four-layered Magnum Board or the rigid foam-cored SIPs.

construction buildings are completed in a single step, as the structure and the flooring surface are made of the same continuous material.

Concrete is ideal for wall systems using slab construction. Other materials, such as metal (corrugated for bending strength) and wood do not have the structural qualities or are not available in the sizes necessary to make slab construction possible without the aid of other materials. Composite materials (7), such as structural insulating panels (SIP), utilise the structural and thermal qualities of different materials sandwiched together (8). Rigid foam insulation is glued to a continuous oriented strand board (OSB) slab construction and sealed around the edges to make well-insulated, airtight panels that are light, easy to handle and capable of supporting loads in the same way as a wooden frame or a brick wall. In effect, they are not so different from light-frame construction, because they employ the same materials but simply take them one step further in the construction process. Like concrete, they lend themselves well to prefabrication and customisation, which is one reason for the growing popularity of this material, especially in the USA.

8

Prefab housing factory
A factory in Marienmünster, Germany, prepares SIPs for shipping. Around 150 mm thick, these boards are light, thin and have insulating and structural strengths required of structural walls.

Post-and-beam construction

The post-and-beam construction is a combination of construction methods. A larger skeletal framework, usually made of steel, reinforced concrete or wood provides the overall structure, and infill panels provide the enclosure (9–11). Structure and surface can be considered independently of one another, allowing a wide range of panel materials (12) to be used and the modules to be varied: they can have different sizes and can be with or without openings, which may also vary in size.

Because the infill panels or materials do not have to carry any loads other than their own, the architect can exercise full freedom of choice. The structural grid can be filled with materials with a variety of colours and textures such as brick skins, aluminium panels, stone cladding or wood, just to name a few. Mies van der Rohe used concrete blocks as infill in the Weißenhofsiedlung in Stuttgart and applied a uniform layer of stucco to cover the structure. The post-and-beam method is more cost-effective for larger projects, such as multi-family housing projects, where there is greater repetition of structural elements. It is therefore not used as frequently for single-family homes.

9

System 01: House E. Kaufmann, Andelsbuch, Austria, Johannes Kaufmann and Oskar Leo Kaufmann, 1997
The system, an example of post-and-beam construction, consists of a laminated-wood skeletal frame and a variety of glazed or wooden wall panels.

10

System 01: House E. Kaufmann, Andelsbuch
A wall panel is lifted into place with a crane.

11

System 01: House E. Kaufmann, Andelsbuch
The finished house.

12

Modern Modular Housing, Penny Collins and Huw Turner, design 2002
The design was conceptualised for the North American market with timber- and metal-framed alternatives for the post-and-beam structure.

On-site building and prefabrication

On-site building

On-site building is the construction of a building and all its elements at the location of the building. Wooden studs are cut and connected, concrete is shuttered and poured in place, and steel beams are welded by hand. It is perceived as a more inefficient way of producing a building when compared to prefabricated housing. However, the working methods in some countries have become highly systemised. One can argue that on-site house production in, say, the USA or the Netherlands, is not only a clear example of system building, but it is also orchestrated and prefabricated as much as its factory-made counterparts (14).

The reduction of required carpentry skills and, consequently, the wages, has resulted in a consequent shortage of trained carpenters in countries such as the USA. The profit-oriented building sector rectified this problem by changing building methods so that the work could be performed using cheap, unskilled labour. Simpson Strong-Tie, one of the leading US manufacturers of metal connectors for wood construction, produces connectors that eliminate measuring and render carpentry knowledge irrelevant (13). Prefabricated steel strap ties, stud shoes, girder truss ties and other wood construction connectors connect, reinforce angles, cover tolerances and eliminate previously necessary woodwork (notches and tongue-and-groove joints) that required highly skilled carpenters. Moreover, the template positioning of nails, positioned to achieve maximum hold without splitting, saves construction time and reduces human errors.

Most homes in North America are on-site light-frame houses, while houses in the Netherlands are mainly prefabricated structures. The fact is that both countries build their homes very systematically, but use a combination of both methods to maximise efficiency. The difference lies in the materials: the majority of

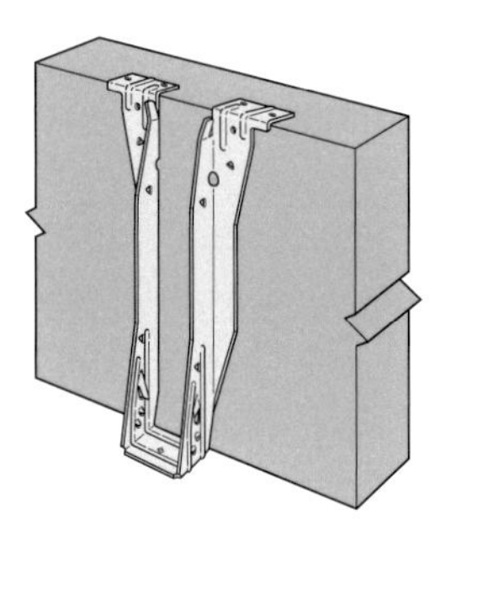

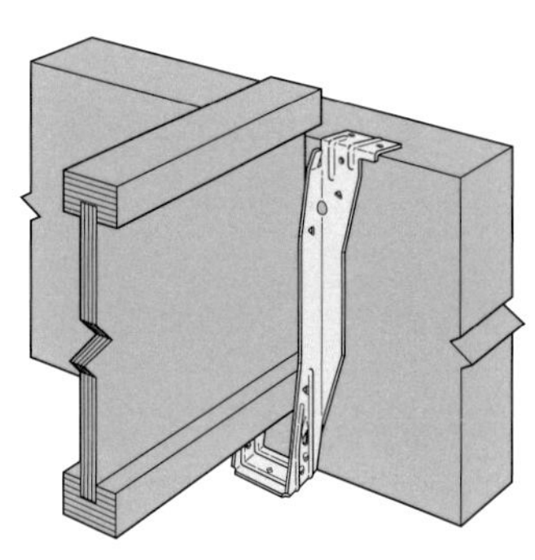

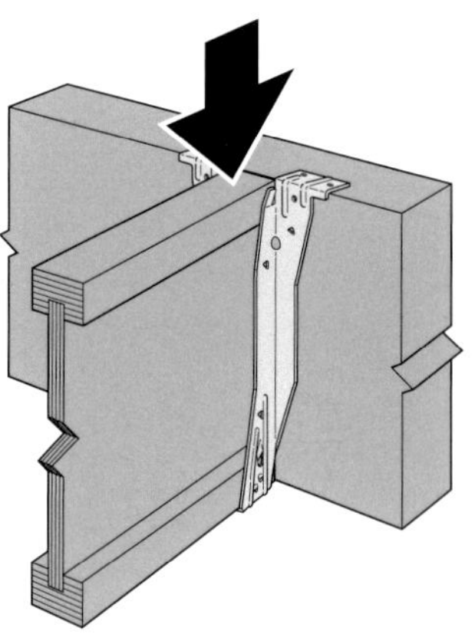

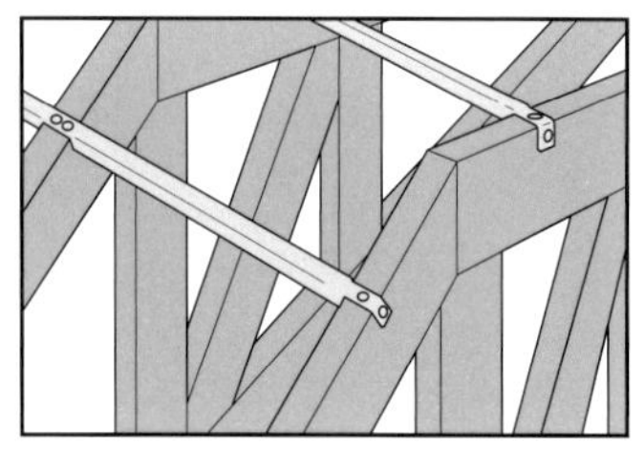

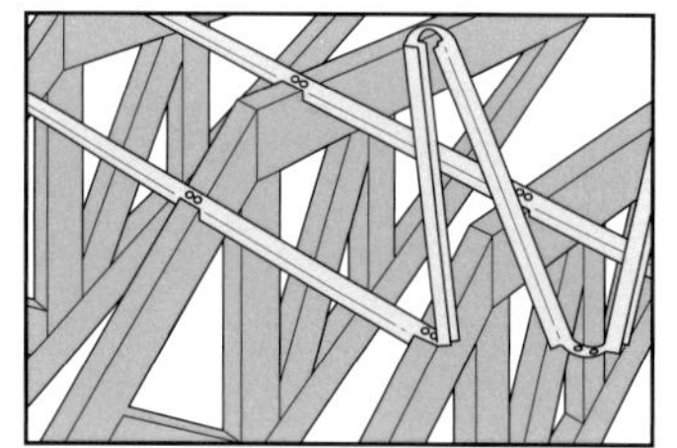

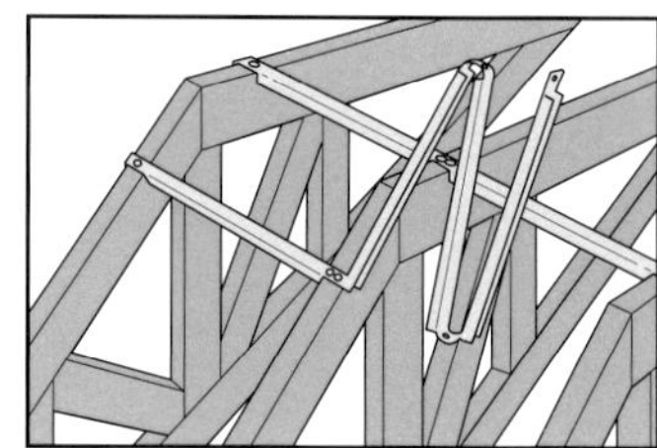

13

Images of installation steps from Simpson Strong-Tie catalogue
The products help eliminate measuring and cutting, save time and reduce the need for skilled labour.

homes in the USA are of wood, while most new homes in the Netherlands are of concrete; as a result the construction methods differ. Homes in the USA are constructed predominantly with the stick-building method, but most of the wood studs, floor joists, flooring panels, doors, windows, matching frames, stairs and roof trusses are precut and delivered to the building site. Much on-site work nevertheless has to be done, as the structure, interior, adjustments and finishes are completed by hand.

Prefabricated concrete elements, not just in the housing sector, have become technically perfected and standardised, so that prefab has become the prevalent method of building in the Netherlands (15). The structure of the houses is often of prefab concrete panels or large concrete blocks. General building practice shows a tendency to complete the remainder of the construction, such as exterior finishes, on site as it is relatively quick and can be controlled individually. The more lenient (in terms of, for instance, fire protection, energy standards or structural requirements) construction standards of both the USA and the Netherlands partly explain why construction is far faster and cheaper in these countries than, for example, in Germany, where slower on-site methods prevail, even with the use of prefabricated elements.

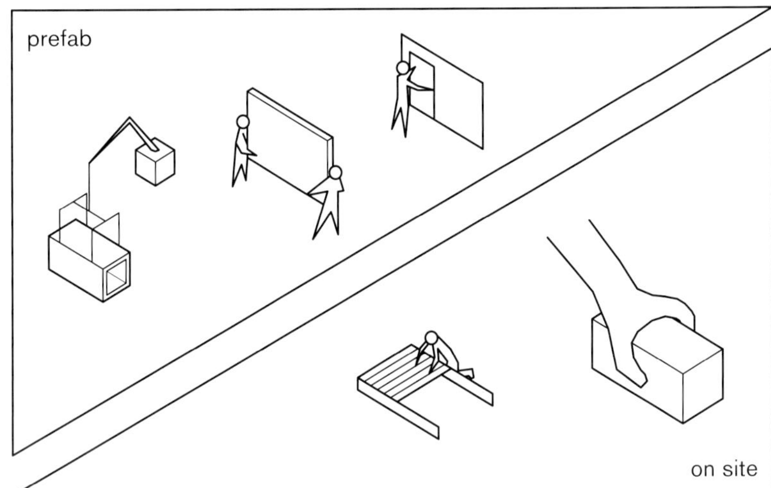

14

Degree of prefabrication and on-site work
There are varying degrees of prefabrication and on-site work. The relationship of prefab and on-site construction is reciprocal, hence more time in the factory equals less time on site and vice versa.

15

House construction in Burgh-Haamstede, the Netherlands
In the Netherlands, the use of a combination of prefabricated and on-site buildings methods alleviates the problems of managing the various trades on site.

Prefabrication

The advantages of prefabrication of building elements in a quality-controlled environment are substantial: the reduction of labour and construction time on the building site, the year-round optimum working conditions of the factory and the precision and overall better quality of the components. The higher costs due to transportation and limitations generally associated with prefabrication outweigh expensive site work, especially in urban areas. As prefabrication speeds up the production process significantly, it allows for earlier capital return, which is often meticulously calculated by large-scale property investors. Prefabrication is therefore a widely adopted practice in both the residential and non-residential sectors. Building family houses in suburban or rural areas usually does not involve the same space limitations as building on urban sites. However, prefabrication is attractive under certain conditions, for example where a high concentration of housing must be erected quickly. Another reason for prefabrication in private housing construction can be attributed to the fixed-price policy of the house building companies, which is a high priority for the client.

Practical application and mass customisation are key goals of standardisation, and standardisation is essential to the production and choice of components. Components such as façade elements or windows and doors, and structural elements such as wooden beams and steel trusses are not only standardised in order to make industrial mass production feasible, but are also coordinated to ease construction and to allow alternatives in design.

Sometimes the meanings and the application of systemisation, prefabrication and standardisation are ambiguous. All-encompassing prefabricated systems such as Kaufmann's System 01 (16, 17) allow unique solutions that standard industrialised products cannot deliver. A prefabricated building quite often includes standard industrialised elements, but a custom-made house made of standard industrialised elements is not necessarily a prefabricated system. A systemised building method, whether it includes standard industrialised elements or not, ensures central quality control.

16

System 01, Johannes Kaufmann and Oskar Leo Kaufmann
The components of the system are built in the factory under ideal conditions.

17

System 01, transport
The dimensions are limited by the width of the road, the vehicle transporting the element and national road traffic regulations.

Flat-pack

If people saw the house as a product that is delivered practically as a do-it-yourself kit of parts, then perhaps the average age of homeowners would decrease drastically. Those opting for the flat-pack system of housing receive the materials directly on site and save on labour costs by erecting the house themselves. A future homeowner could alternatively hire an architect, get the plans approved, and build the home from standard, industrialised parts himself, but with a flat-pack house, he can do away with the planning part and simply get on with the work. A variety of design solutions are available for different needs.

Flat-pack is the prefab answer for the young or those gifted with handyman skills (18, 19). The name flat-pack refers to the way in which the system components are delivered to the owner – as precut flat panels compactly stacked together. In this way, the building components are built in the factory, efficiently packed to save space, delivered and finally assembled on site.

Since 2004, the Japanese home and lifestyle company Muji has been offering ready-designed houses; one of the three available types was designed by Kazuhiko Namba (20). The Muji Houses are marketed on the same platforms as the home furnishings. The "simple and good quality" principle of Muji and the do-it-yourself concept of IKEA both work well with the ready-designed (although not quite ready-made) principle of flat-pack home delivery. In Japan as well as in Sweden, home of the IKEA BoKlok House, prefabricated housing accounts for 90 % of all housing, and the designs maintain the simplicity of traditional homes.

18

DIY House, San Francisco, California, Endres Ware, 2007
The flat-pack house can be built by amateurs with simple tools within two weeks.

19

DIY House, San Francisco
The house is designed to fit into typically long semi-urban plots and accommodate customers with an average income and a modern lifestyle.

20

Muji + Infill house, Japan, Kazuhiko Namba, 2004
Displayed among other minimalist designed products at a Muji store in Japan, the life-sized prefabricated demonstration house is showcased alongside such products as furniture, bath articles, office products and clothing.

Modular building

Since the advent of modern prefabrication, modular building no longer refers only to the practice of building to a standard dimensional module, but also to the prefabrication of a volumetric building unit. Modules are three-dimensional independent units or partially complete sections. They can be repeated by stacking or joining side by side in order to extend spaces. The module is the most complete form of prefabrication, usually about 95 % fully fitted with the essential kitchen and bathroom facilities, storage amenities and living spaces in the factory, and then sealed for transportation. The greatest advantage of modular building is that the building is immediately ready for use after power and water facilities are connected.

Compared to other types of prefabrication, this is the most cumbersome and technically challenging one due to the transport of enclosed usable space. Their weight is limited by the load capacity of trucks, trains or helicopters, and the size of the modules is limited by road widths and shipping container standards, while the maximum width not requiring special permission for road transport is 2.55 m. The modules are usually lifted into place by cranes and bolted in position. During lifting, the modules are subjected to structural forces, notably vertical bending and shear, which are quite different to those they experience after installation. The need to strengthen the modules for lifting and the doubling of floor, roof and wall frames at the connection points result in greater quantities of structural material.

21

Spacebox, Delft, the Netherlands, Mart de Jong/DeVijf, 2003
The stackable container-like student housing produced by Holland Composite offers a delightful and uncomplicated solution to the urgent need for student housing.

22

Loftcube, Berlin, Werner Aisslinger, 2007
The luxurious boxed room has a floor space of up to 39 m^2 and can be used as a vacation home or an additional penthouse space in the city.

Trailer homes, still popular in the USA since their uptake in the 1930s, are basically modules on wheels. Such manufactured homes are the answer to the industrialisation of the house as a product. The equally futuristic notion of living in capsules became a reality in the 1970s with the Nakagin Capsules in Tokyo (Kisho Kurokawa, 1972) and the Capsule Hotel (Kisho Kurokawa, 1979) in Osaka. Both examples are in Japan, where the real estate prices are so high that tight living spaces are the norm. The most basic examples of modular building are shipping containers, fitted out with the proper insulation and services and stacked upon each other or within a framework, as temporary forms of living such as students' quarters (21) or asylum seekers' accommodation. The level of comfort ranges from bare and loud to luxurious and solitary, but the concept of living in a box, at least temporarily, can have a certain aesthetic appeal (22).

In the extension of the Post Hotel in Bezau (23, 24), Austria, the advantages of building with modules clearly outweigh the disadvantages. Firstly, extremely cold weather conditions and mountainous terrain would have greatly hindered continuous assembly. Secondly, on-site construction had to be kept to a minimum because of the year-round opening times of this highly-ranked hotel for winter athletes and spa visitors. Thirdly, the high level of craftsmanship of the interiors required specific machinery and precise control. In this case, the travelling distance was only 2 km and the independent floor and ceiling systems offered an excellent sound barrier for the hotel guests.

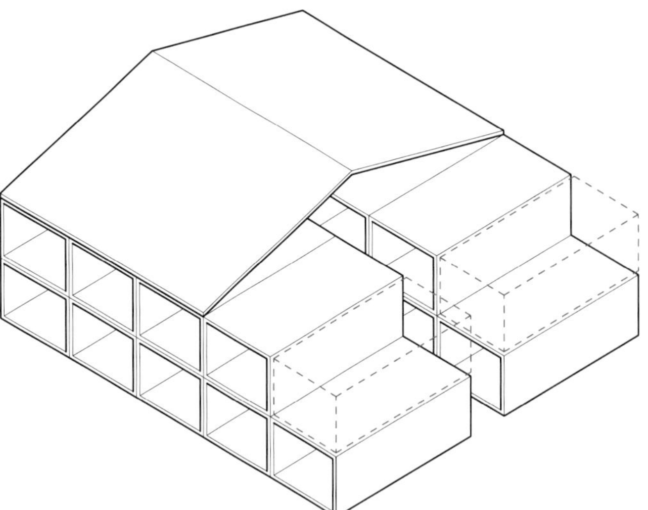

23

Post Hotel extension, Bezau, Austria, Oskar Leo Kaufmann and Albert Ruf, 1998
Building modules are the most complete form of prefabrication. The modules are completely fitted out, lifted into place by a crane and connected to power and water facilities.

24

Post Hotel extension, Bezau
The system consists of a framework, hotel modules and a roof for protection.

Culture and the issue of design

USA

The choice of architectural styles of housing in the USA is vast. The style mostly used for light-frame building is a modified version of the vernacular or traditional US house: porch, façade with neo-classical ornaments and pitched roof. The highly efficient method of light-frame building is a systemised process and hence part of system building, although the actual construction work takes place on site. A house that is categorised as prefabricated, on the other hand, is firmly linked to modern architecture, i.e. minimalist design and usually a flat roof. This, too, is built using building system techniques as most people would define them – but mainly in the factory.

Stick-frame houses

Remarkably, over 95 % of new homeowners in the USA have never spoken to an architect, mostly because they own contractor-made stick-frame homes, but also because the housing industry does well without architects. Almost all wood and steel elements, connections, façade components and components such as stairs, roofing systems and mechanical systems are standardised and industrially produced. Style features such as gables, columns, porticos and endless types of façade veneers are pasted on the main structure like masks. Previously considered an unsystematic, inefficient system of building, on-site construction has become a highly organised system, capable of churning out a traditional-looking house in less than a month.

The simple application of design to a stick-frame house allows US homeowners to get what they want – space and technical comfort on the inside and the "home" look on the outside – for an affordable price. Houses are almost always presented as variable products with a resale value in the real estate market. However varied the styles may be, the overwhelming tendency toward the traditional building type is painstakingly uncreative. Styles are loosely tagged as, for example, Georgian, Spanish Colonial, Mediterranean, Victorian and Greek Revival, and there is even the option to compromise with a melange of styles (26).

Quadrant Homes is one of the most profitable housing companies in the USA and owes its success to its adaptation of Eiji Toyoda's lean principles. Founded in Seattle in 1969, the company sold over 1,000 houses in 2003 alone, producing over 250 million USD in revenue. Prior to 1996, Quadrant produced and stored building elements (build-to-stock strategy); today the company produces when the orders come in. The firm uses an appealing marketing strategy, and homeowners are offered choice, quality and the security of various structural, technical

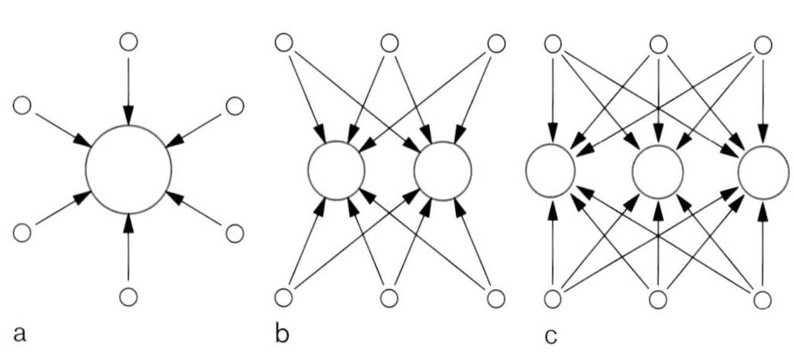

25

The house-building industry in different countries
Whereas the centralised housing industry prevalent in Japan (a) is more efficiently controlled, the balanced relationship of housing developers and contractors in countries such as the Netherlands or the USA (b) offers more options of quality. The decentralised relationship (c) prevalent in Germany and Austria is diversified and supports the individual builder.

26

Windermere, Forsyth County, Georgia
700 homes sprouted in this finely groomed housing development, which began on site in 2002. A patchwork of derivations of borrowed style elements on one street, or even on one house, is not uncommon.

and environmental warranties. Advanced software makes customising easy. Each house, built in the wood framing method on site, takes 54 days to build. The workload is scheduled in such a way that every construction stage is synchronised at six houses per day. This example of system building is effectively an inverse assembly line – the different stages of the "factory" move from house to house.

Prefabricated housing

Eye-catching websites on prefabricated housing like www.fabprefab.com and www.prefabs.com are spreading the trend in modern architecture, which was previously limited to the design-conscious (28, 29). Insiders seek inspiration through trendsetters like *Dwell* magazine. American designers like Michelle Kaufmann, Rocio Romero (27), Marmol Radziner and Associates are well-known names to prefab aficionados. The Internet provides the potential homeowner (prefab or not) with choices of materials, arrangements and sizes, and when they have finished shopping, they can ring up the total price, usually not including foundations and public utilities. Fabprefab, a platform for both on-the-market and potential prefab homes from all over the world, proves that the interest in prefab exists on a global scale.

27

LV Series Home, Perryville, Missouri, Rocio Romero, 2000
The minimalistic LV Series Home is factory-built as a kit of parts. It is built with steel posts and OSB panels, a simple, durable, green and cost-effective solution with scope for many design and technical options.

How do architects go about conceptualising, developing, marketing and building the prefab house in the USA? The business of prefabricated architecture is challenging.

Typically, an architect comes up with a design, finds a contractor to fund and build a prototype and then finds a developer to manufacture the product. Another strategy places the developer as the central figure. The developer, more experienced with real estate fluctuations and usually backed up with more capital, brings in the architect to design a house system and a builder to produce the system components, has a prototype built and organises the marketing strategy. A prefab home builder, Living Homes of Santa Monica, California, for example, works with this strategy, featuring two or three architects and promising the necessary expertise in building and management. Another company, Parco Homes, is run by an architect with a team of experts from

28

Abiquiu House, Abiquiu, New Mexico, Anderson Anderson Architecture, 2009
The house was built with readily available prefabricated elements and industrial products – however, it is not strictly a prefab house but rather a one-off design.

the real estate, business management and engineering fields. In this way, the prefabricated house system is designed and developed while all the other aspects of the product including production and marketing are pursued, thus ensuring quality control. Consistent with all strategies is that the architect cannot produce the prefab product alone; the architect needs a business companion because the prefab house is a factory product and requires much more than a good design in order to sell (30).

29

Johnson Creek weeHouse, Honesdale, Pennsylvania, Alchemy Architects, 2008
The weeHouse design is based on fully fitted modules the size of a shipping container. Since 2002, some 20 houses of this type – with varying façade materials and module combinations – have been built.

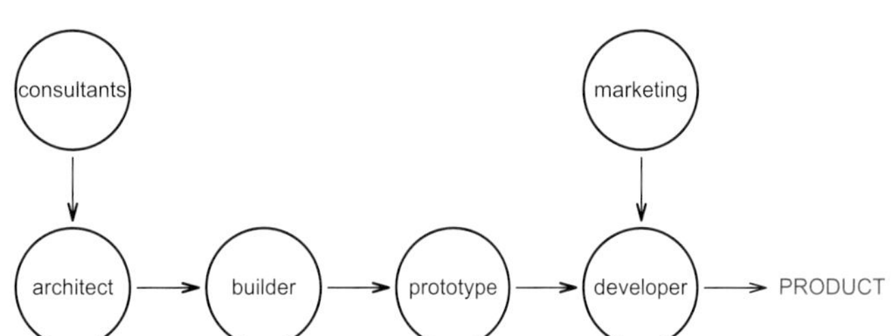

a Linear strategy

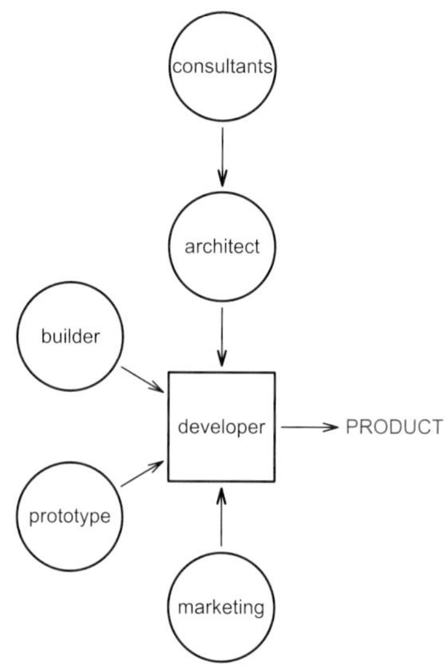

b Centralised strategy with developer as central figure (Example: Living Homes)

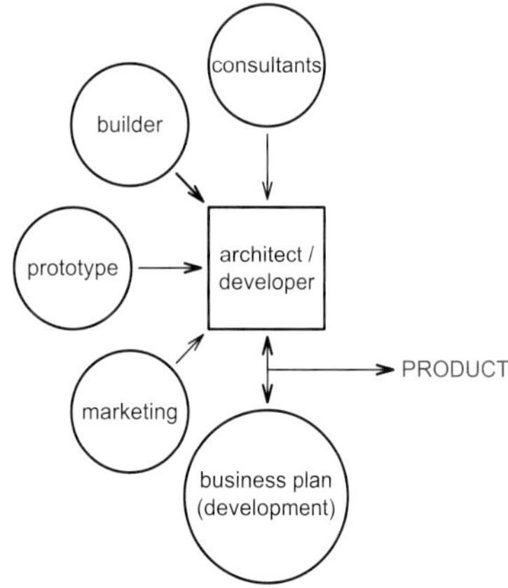

c Centralised strategy with architect and developer as central figure (Example: Parco Homes)

30

Strategies for marketing the prefabricated house
The marketing strategies for prefab houses with linear (a) and centralised (b, c) options of development.

The Netherlands

The Dutch have reclaimed thousands of hectares of land from under the Zuider Zee since the 1930s and have maintained very progressive government policies for urban planning. The national planning policies have ensured that not only housing, but also economic activities, land and water conservation and infrastructure are balanced. One of the most inspiring achievements is the number of housing units subsidised and built by the government since the Second World War – about 80 % of the present housing stock of 7 million. This could not have been possible without the consistent use and development of prefabricated, industrialised building components.

The population of 16 million is relatively small, but there is little usable land space, since 61 % is used for agriculture and 19 % is covered by water. The density of 483 inhabitants per square kilometre is greater than that of Japan (323/km²), which has similar compactly built areas. This illustrates the good sense of the Bijlmermeer, or "bundled concentration" called for by Dutch law. Two thirds of the nation's 7 million homes are attached houses, most of the rest are in low-rise apartment buildings and very few are single-family homes. This differs greatly from the single-family home dominated suburbs of America, and from the much higher density of high-rises of the rest of Europe. In comparison, 53 % of Germans live in apartment buildings and most others live in single-family homes.

Traditional styles are not as prevalent as in the USA. Dutch homeowners and tenants (about 35 % of homes are social rental houses, mostly owned and managed by housing associations) have been much more open to experiments in architecture (31). Up until the 1990s, most of the housing components were prefabricated on such a large scale that the repetition of houses became monotonous. However, thanks to government housing subsidies, architects and planners were able to develop systems of building, mostly of concrete, that substantially alleviated the on-site construction process, saved time and money and allowed for variations. A fresh wave of architectural experiments sprouted in settlements like Almere, one of the new towns and growth centres created outside existing cities as so-called greenfield developments since the 1960s to ease the densification of the old centres. Since its beginnings in 1975, Almere grew from a handful to 180,000 inhabitants and can boast many clever ideas in architecture (32).

31

Residential development Woonhof De Dolphijn, Middelburg, the Netherlands, Fierloos Architecten, 2002
The tight juxtaposition of identical homes is typical of Dutch housing developments.

32

Typical housing development in Almere, the Netherlands
This generation-old town showcases many architectural experiments and unconventional solutions to house its 180,000 inhabitants.

33

Sorest Home Model, Toyota Homes
These modular homes are built on the assembly line in a housing plant and assembled on site within 45 days. Like most housing companies in Japan, Toyota homes range in size, style and price and offer other amenities, such as a recharging system for eco-friendly hybrid cars.

Japan

Along with the Netherlands and Sweden, Japan is one of the major hubs of prefabrication with 90 % of all single-family homes (1.25 million homes per year) coming from the factory (25). A handful of large diversified firms, often rising out of other industries (like Mitsui, Sekisui Chemical and supermarket chains) have included prefabricated housing in their programme and account for almost all prefabricated homes built in Japan in the last decades (33). Home exhibitions in Japan display houses made from precast concrete, structural steel, timber-frame as well as light-gauge steel and wooden light-frame construction. Fully automated home factories like Daiwa use both robotics and manpower to prefabricate a complete house within an astonishing five hours. Engineered construction details like continuous joints and the general efficiency of material use can be attributed to prefabrication, especially in situations where traditional architecture would have called for complex, difficult-to-construct wooden joints. Earthquake-proof Mitsui Isolation Systems go one step farther by easing the stress of fixed joints through ball-bearing motion-dampening systems at foundation level. Moreover, state-of-the-art entertainment facilities, sensitivity-controlled living environments as well as technology learned from the auto industry, such as electricity-producing fuel cells and vibration dampers, are being applied to the housing product. The prefab home building company Sekisui, which erects 56,000 units a year, developed the Zero Emission House in 2008 as an environmentally conscious solution.

Two main aspects characterise system-built housing in Japan: the modularisation of building components based on traditional Japanese architecture and technical engineering fostered by years of production ideals. Traditional building used the tatami mat and column spacing as dimensional modules to facilitate the production and interchangeability of building components. Permanence was not important, but the material was. Spaces were shifted through sliding doors, and the option of dismantling and relocating a building was a device in case of war, or today, of natural disaster. The steel-framed houses produced by Daiwa House Group are still based on the tatami mat grid. Houses today do not need to be designed to be dismantled, but the company, always adapting to customers' changing needs, is currently developing changeable frames and interiors in response to the country's changing demographics. As in most westernised countries, families have decreased in size.

Constant change is the underlying factor in the appearance of the home. The house is a sign of stability in the society, yet with an average 25-year lifespan, it is as tenuous a product as the automobile or a laptop. Factory-made houses in Japan, like cars and electronics, are controlled, mass-produced manufactured products and are more accepted than in North America and much of Europe. Stylistically, the home exteriors adapt trendy western elements, but with the exception of a few minimalistic architect-designed prefab homes, there is little innovation in the sea of indistinctive architecture. For most, the emphasis is rather on the spatial organisation of the sacred private interior, as the traditional house court and modern living room reflect, and guaranteed good building standards. The focus of architectural critics is the emergence of the few architect-designed homes with a utilitarian aesthetic for embracing bold forms and visually extending spaces with light. The F.O.B. Houses, developed and marketed by a large household goods retail chain, the F.O.B. Co-op, are a case in point. They offer individual, affordable designs with contemporary exteriors by using consistent detailing and cooperating with the same few building companies (34, 35).

34

Um House, Ikoma, Nara Prefecture, Japan, F.O.B. Architecture, 2000
The F.O.B. Houses offer individual, affordable designs with contemporary exteriors. The homes are not restricted to specific modules or materials and can be built of concrete, wood or steel.

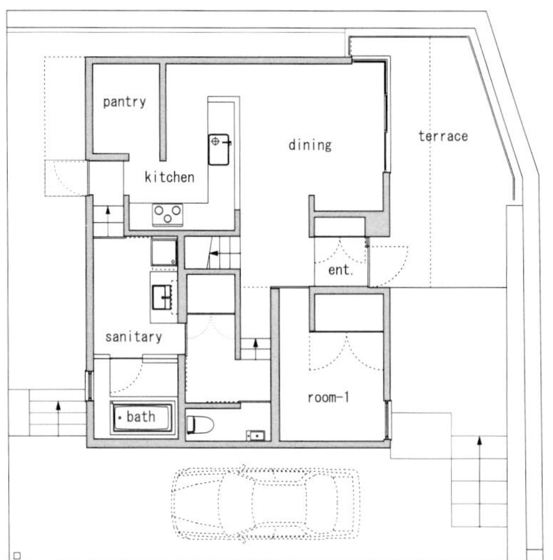

Ground floor plan

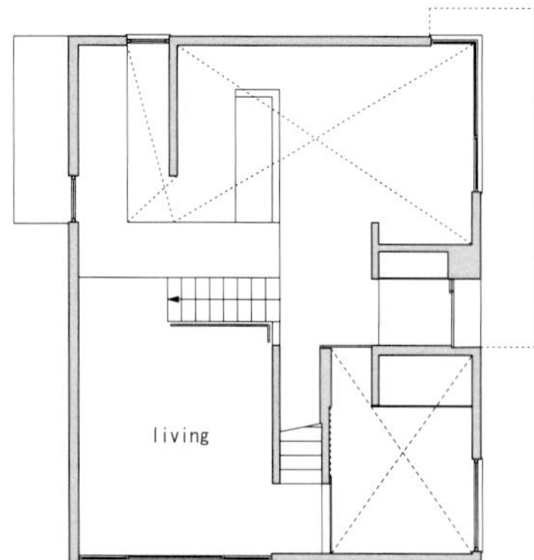

First floor plan

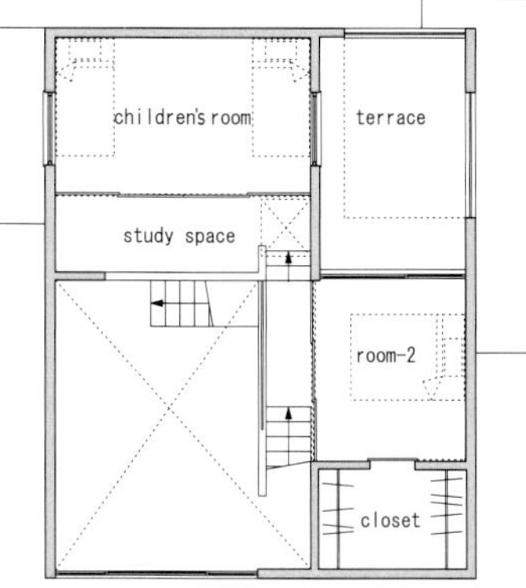

Second floor plan

35

Um House, Ikoma
The Um House is one of five prototypes of F.O.B. Houses developed on principles of spatial continuity and interior courtyards, both reminders of the traditional Japanese house.

Great Britain

Martin Pawley stated in *A Private Future* 30 years ago that housing was a product in a consumer society. The vast majority of people in Great Britain rented their houses under terms of tenure, an oppressive condition in contrast to the privilege of ownership. The negative image of rental housing was directly associated with post-war era prefabrication and lasted for decades as much of the temporary housing became permanent. There was a problematic duality from the beginning; the hype to own everything from gadgets to cars spoke for industrial production of all things necessary, but when it came to housing, it had to be built with traditional methods and be affordable at the same time. The numbers have reversed since then: in 2009, 17.5 million, or roughly 80 % of British dwellings were owner-occupied. But the resistance to prefabrication still persists from both the consumer as well as from the housebuilder.

The reasons for consumer resistance to prefabricated building, also referred to as off-site MMC (modern methods of construction) are manifold: financing a prefabricated home is difficult because lenders find new materials a risk. Obtaining permissions to build is known to be complicated, and land is scarce and pricey. The primary generator of resistance, ironically, lies in the nature of owner-occupation, in which the home is primarily an investment, rather than a consumer good or a living environment. This means that people will pay more to ensure higher future value, so a house must have the right location, be durable (i.e. of brick or granite) and, very importantly, not look prefabricated. Accordingly, the clients are resistant to new materials, technology and non-standard forms.

The Egan Report *Rethinking Construction* (1998), one of the most influential initiatives aimed at improving the efficiency and quality of the construction industry, instigated research into the prefabrication of homes. The highly fragmented building industry, however, has failed to adopt a greater degree of prefabrication and standardisation of processes and products. The reasons for this include high capital cost, the difficulty to achieve economies of scale, complex interfacing between systems, and the nature of the British planning system. Off-site methods amongst larger private-sector developers are applied to a very limited extent, but are growing. The advantages are clear: compensation for shortages of skilled labour, time and cost certainty,

36

Oxley Woods housing site, Milton Keynes, Great Britain, Rogers Stirk Harbour + Partners, 2008
A concept for low-cost prefabricated housing units with a modular palette of forms that can be adapted to today's changing demographics. The Trespa cladding panels, made of thermosetting resins and wood fibres, are an example of the conscious choice of materials with an integrated environmental management system (EcoHat).

higher quality and minimised on-site duration. The products today are of marginal quality, and this is worsened by the downsized spaces governed by developers.

Entirely prefabricated homes make up a tiny fraction of the British home industry, but this market is growing. Among others, the Murray Grove urban renewal housing project with one of the first manufactured prefab modular homes in Great Britain by Cartwright Pickard Architects (2000) of London and the affordable BoKlok House by IKEA (1997) of Sweden have caught the attention of potential homeowners in a climate of high demand for housing. A particularly interesting project, the Oxley Woods housing site in Milton Keynes by Rogers Stirk Harbour + Partners shows a shift in the needs of the homeowner and subsequent new wind in architectural style (36). This project was commissioned by central government after a competition for low-cost prefabricated housing and has reached excellent energy rating standards. The palette of forms is modular and simple, untypical in the neighbourhood, and continues a trend set by persevering architects of all generations. The variable modular cladding panels can be adapted to suit the various needs of the owners. Changing lifestyles and the increasing emphasis on sustainability, coupled with good prices, make this innovative mass housing prototype a success. These benefits are achieved through a carefully engineered manufacturing process together with the cladding design concept and efficient living and servicing zones. The EcoHat, a rooftop service unit, reduces energy consumption by almost 40 % by providing passive solar water heating, filtering fresh air and recovering the heat from the circulating air (37).

37

EcoHat, Milton Keynes, Great Britain, Rogers Stirk, Harbour + Partners, 2008
The EcoHat is a service unit on top of the roof of the Oxley Woods houses. It reduces energy consumption by almost 40 % by providing passive solar water heating, filtering fresh air and recovering the heat from the circulating air.

Austria

For the houses in Vorarlberg, a mountainous region in the western tip of Austria, a thin line lies between the vernacular and the modern (40). There exists not a competition of styles or building types, but generations of gradual modifications of the traditional building type, which accommodate modern domestic needs with newer building methods. When one looks at the vernacular buildings of the area, one sees farm houses of compact form, built of solid wood with pitched roofs, wooden shingles and clay roof tiles. The newer houses of the area have the same sturdy structural qualities, but there are occasional flat roofs, metal cladding and other new materials, subtle sculpting of form, larger windows and an open plan interior. The changes appear to be slight, but modernism is obvious.

38

SU-SI House, Reuthe, Austria, Oskar Leo Kaufmann and Johannes Kaufmann, 1998
A prefabricated modular home built as a prototype for more systems to follow. The architect, the client and the builder are all in the same family.

39

Interior of SU-SI House, Reuthe
The modular home is a complete entity – it is fitted out with space-saving amenities with simple, clear details.

The accommodation of smaller families, integrated workspaces and energy-saving solutions has led to an optimisation of construction systems. The resulting architecture itself is most impressive – it is not a sudden modern architecture but one that is rooted; the lines and connections are clean, details are slick and for the most part, the gestalt is elegant and refined. As architect Johannes Kaufmann of Bregenz, puts it, "the Bregenzers have had the same basic features for 300 years", despite phases during the post-war period where concrete replaced wood as the predominant building material. His observation is that the boundaries between occupations such as carpenter, cabinetmaker, builder and architect are disappearing. There is less hierarchy between the professions than in the USA or other parts of Europe. As in Switzerland, a wide-spread awareness of the building environment exists. In the Vorarlberg region roughly 50% of the houses are built by architects, something American, German, British and Japanese architects can only dream about. Affordability, design and superb quality exist thanks to problem-oriented thinking: in the mountainous terrain and cold weather, the prefabrication of building components in the factory is a logical way to build consistently and well. And, there is perhaps the human aspect to it – the architects and builders see architecture, simply and respectfully, as a passion.

The value of carpentry is also a tradition in the area – carpentry is a highly regarded profession and the carpenters' involvement in the production of good architecture is direct as they work closely with architects. Michael Kaufmann of Reuthe in Vorarlberg, for one, is a third generation manager of a wood manufacturing company that produces systems and custom-made wood products (38, 39). Together with other family members in the industry, he has built system building components as flat-pack, modular and hybrid systems. The job requires years of apprenticeship and schooled qualifications. In return, the system of effective production with highly skilled craftsmen makes the product more affordable.

40

House F., Bezau, Austria, Dietrich Untertrifaller Architekten, 2006
This contemporary architecture references both in form and choice of materials the Bregenzerwaldhaus, the traditional farm house of the Bregenzerwald region.

4 | Systems in Industrial Buildings

This chapter discusses complete building systems in terms of their characteristics as modular systems, as well as buildings and projects that can be generally placed under the headings of prefabrication and standardisation. A complete system is a building that is provided as a whole unit by a single manufacturer. Standardised building, on the other hand, is based on the use of prefabricated components. This is an important criterion and a feature that distinguishes standardised building from complete systems.

Systems and standardised building for offices and industrial buildings encompass a very wide field of use. The spectrum of all the different construction types and building processes can be best explained in terms of these uses. The construction types of industrial buildings – be they erected as system buildings or using standardised building components – can be divided into the categories ultra-lightweight, modular, steel skeleton, mixed concrete/steel skeleton and concrete skeleton buildings (1).

Ultra-lightweight

Ultra-lightweight buildings include lightweight glass and membrane structures such as tents, glass and plastic film (polythene) greenhouses. This category also covers long-span roofs, for example over sports stadia and railway stations. Their low mass is due to a lightweight outer skin and a minimal loadbearing structure, which normally restricts their height to a single storey. The overwhelming majority of systems in this category are designed to provide temporary buildings, for which a low weight, compact dimensions when packed away for transport, and ease of erection and disassembly are important.

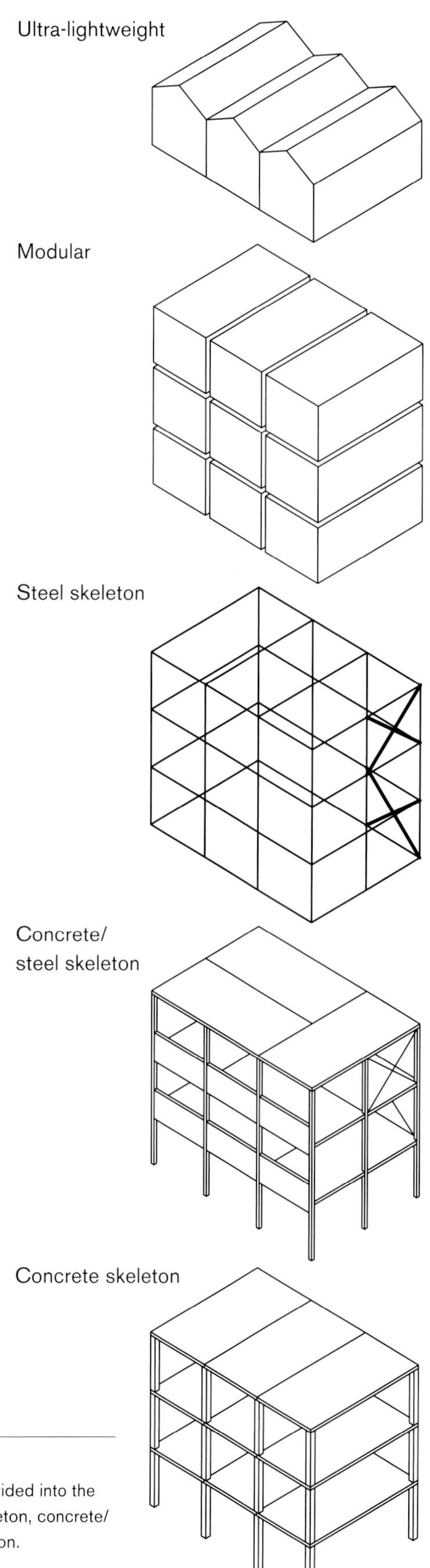

1

Industrial building construction types
Industrial building construction types can be divided into the categories ultra-lightweight, modular, steel skeleton, concrete/steel skeleton and concrete skeleton construction.

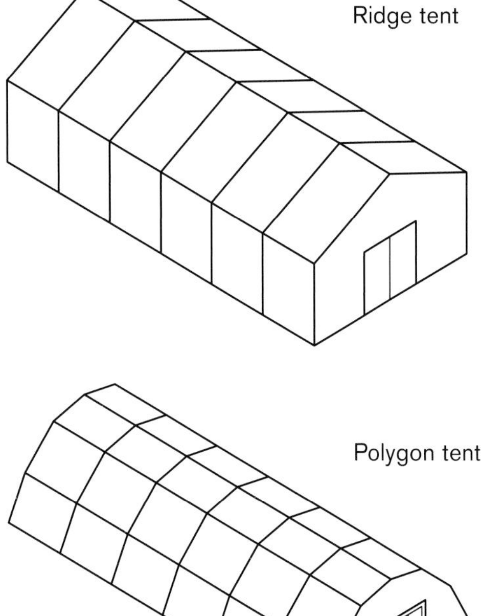

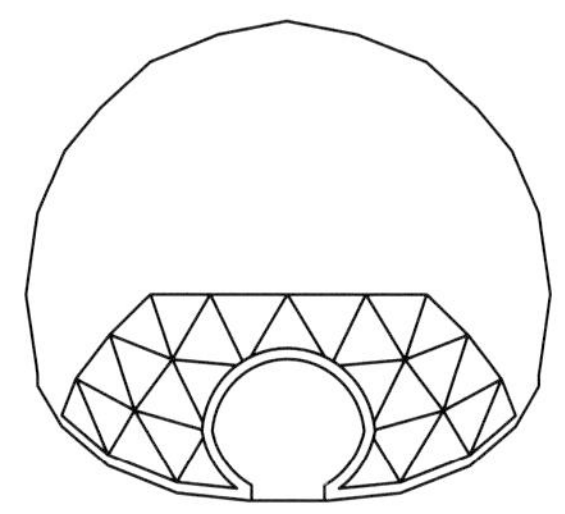

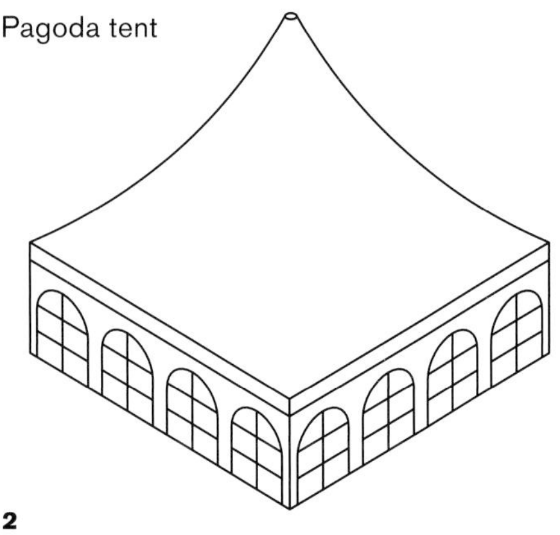

2

Tent systems
The most popular form of tent is the ridge tent. Other tent forms in popular use include polygon, dome and pagoda tents.

Tent systems

Tents are the oldest form of system building. Developed by nomadic populations as portable accommodation, they are still used today for their transportability and ease of assembly and disassembly as temporary buildings, above all for storage facilities, buildings for social events and commercial exhibitions, as well as for emergency accommodation and relief shelters following disasters (2).

Ridge tents

The traditional ridge tent is the most popular tent type for commercial uses. The pneumatic roof structure is an interesting further development of this tent type. This form of construction has loadbearing advantages in addition to providing improved thermal insulation (3).

Dome tents

The technology of the transportable big tent for events, such as circus "big tops" and mirror tents developed for example in the Netherlands and Belgium, first emerged at the end of the 19th century. With these event tents, it is important that the interior remains as clear of intermediate supports as possible, so that there is complete freedom in the choice of layout and visitors have an unobstructed view of the space. Richard Buckminster Fuller developed the geodesic dome, a very light, strong and simple structure based on a modular dome system, in the 1950s (7). Based on this idea, the young Berlin company Zendome developed a dome tent system for events (4–6). The Zendome system offers event tents up to 1000 m^2 in area.

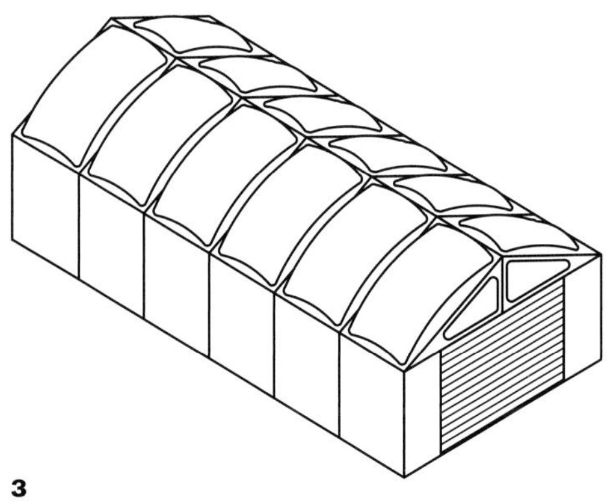

3

Ridge tent with air cushion roof
The roof can be made of air cushions to improve thermal insulation.

4

Geodesic dome tent, Zendome: external view
The special feature of this tent system is its special dome structure, which has particularly good structural properties.

5

Geodesic dome tent: internal view
The dome shape is formed from a modular, geodesic loadbearing structure made up of equilateral triangles.

6

Geodesic dome tent: loadbearing structure
Detail of the ultra-lightweight strut structure, which relies on the space-grid action of its members.

The special feature of this tent system is its dome, which consists of a modular, geodesic loadbearing structure made up of equilateral triangles. Only two basic elements are required to construct the dome: a scaffold tube with node plates with bolt holes at its ends, which can be bolted to others by means of node discs to form a loadbearing structure of triangular panels. The scaffold tubes are powder-coated galvanised steel. A textile membrane, a polyester fabric coated on both sides with PVC, is pulled over the loadbearing structure to create an external skin.

The construction of the tent dome is more complex and expensive than other comparable forms of tent types and less flexible in tent sizes. Its advantage over other tent systems lies in the structural engineering options offered by this type of structure. The low self-weight allows large interiors, uninterrupted by intermediate supports, to be provided on a temporary basis. The loadbearing structure is very stiff in reaction to wind loads, and event equipment or furnishings can be suspended from the internal steel grid construction.

Modular systems

Modular buildings are steel lightweight building systems assembled out of self-supporting modules. There are two categories: container and module systems. Container building systems are based on the idea of the standard ISO transport containers used worldwide with great success in modular goods transport systems. The construction, size and form of container building modules are directly derived from the transport container industry. Container buildings can be reused many times. In addition to being sold outright, they are also leased temporarily to their users (8).

Modular building systems are built to similar dimensions and construction principles as container modules. Modular units are therefore equally easy to transport but have a higher level of design quality than container module systems. The greatest difference compared with container systems is the possibility of customisation of the individual modules. They are generally used for more sophisticated purposes and for longer periods. Modular buildings can be seen as an intermediate step towards customised permanent building systems. Modular buildings are not only sold by the manufacturer, they can also be leased. In modular building systems, complete building modules based on a self-supporting steel frame are prefabricated and completely fitted out in a factory. On site they are put together like building blocks, in accordance with the layout plans, to form a complete building (11). After the modules have been connected together on site to form the basic building, the open joints between the modules internally, in the façade and on the roof are sealed, and the individual ancillary components, such as stairwells or lifts, are installed on site.

Hospital extensions are one of the fields in which these systems are used with success. Advantages such as the speed and relative ease of construction, and an uncluttered site compared with the conventional on-site methods, are particularly important here. Many companies all over the world offer modular systems. The differences are generally in the company's ability to provide various sizes and designs of modules.

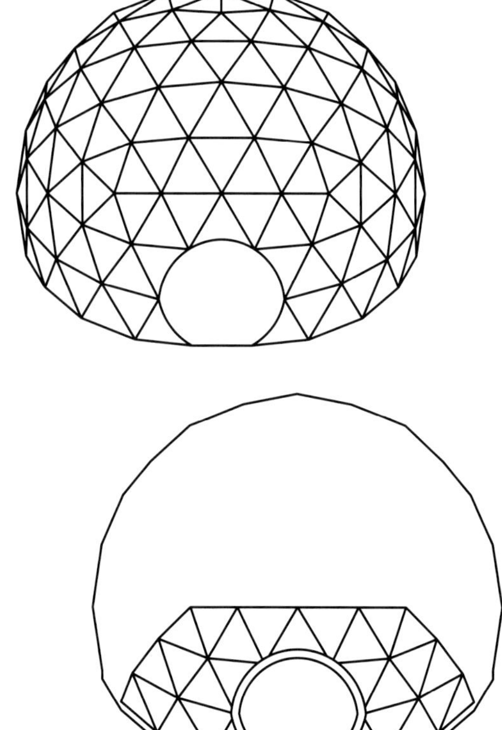

7

Diagram illustrating the loadbearing structure of a geodesic dome
The geometry is formed from triangles.

Container systems

Office and sanitary containers base their dimensions on those of the standard ISO container. Container systems are used as office and sanitary containers in a wide range of fields, for example site offices, nursery schools and other educational establishments.

Container systems closely follow the principles of lightweight construction (10). The design is derived from the construction of shipping containers and motor vehicles. The chassis is usually a steel frame bolted together from cold-rolled steel profiles. The walls consist of insulated lightweight panels. The frame and panels can be designed to fit into flat packs, e.g. Transpack containers for transport (9). This approach, in which the corner columns and the wall panels are all contained within the flat packs, cuts down shipping volumes considerably. The containers can be moved and set up on site by a crane or fork-lift truck.

8

Container systems used as site facilities
The modular construction of container systems is plain to see, for example, in the site facilities for the new Elbphilharmonie concert hall in Hamburg.

9

Transporting containers as flat packs
Containers can be folded down into a space-saving flat pack to avoid having to transport empty space.

The size of a container is generally referred to as its nominal length in feet. The international container sizes are 20-foot (6.09 × 2.44 × 2.60 m) and 40-foot modules (12.19 × 2.44 × 2.60 m). Many European companies' container systems are also aligned to this international system. Container modules can be brought together to form large building complexes. The maximum storey height of container buildings is limited by structural engineering considerations. Wind loads, which increase with every additional storey, limit the scope of combination of container modules. Greater numbers of storeys mean more walls to stiffen the structure as a whole. Different systems allow container modules to be combined in different ways (12).

Containers can be found all over the world in use as temporary building systems. They perform very efficiently over the whole period of construction and use: the consistent adoption of the ISO container sizes means transport is very flexible, making use of existing equipment already designed to handle international standard ISO containers all over the world. Container modules can be manufactured in a factory before being dispatched and set up with very little extra work. Because they can be disassembled back to individual modules again without suffering damage and transported away, they are suitable for many successive reuses. Storing them poses no problems, as each container has its own roof and outside walls, making a storage warehouse unnecessary.

Container buildings are specialist building systems that depend on transportability. This sets limits on their use. Disadvantages of this consistently adopted design philosophy include the fixed volume and dimensions of the modules, the almost mandatory use of lightweight materials and construction, and the low thermal storage capacity of the buildings. They are therefore hardly ever called upon to fulfil any role beyond their temporary tasks and become, for example, residential buildings or permanent office buildings.

A tower of 17 recycled overseas containers, which had been customised specifically for this building, was designed to house the offices and showroom of Freitag lab AG (13). The standard container is a standalone, structurally optimised system. So in a case like this, where the external skin was interrupted by stairs and large façade openings, strengthening measures were necessary inside the containers themselves. The containers are otherwise self-contained and are linked to one another only by the sort of frictional fittings used in shipbuilding. They can also be replaced in the future. Wind loads are transferred to the founda-

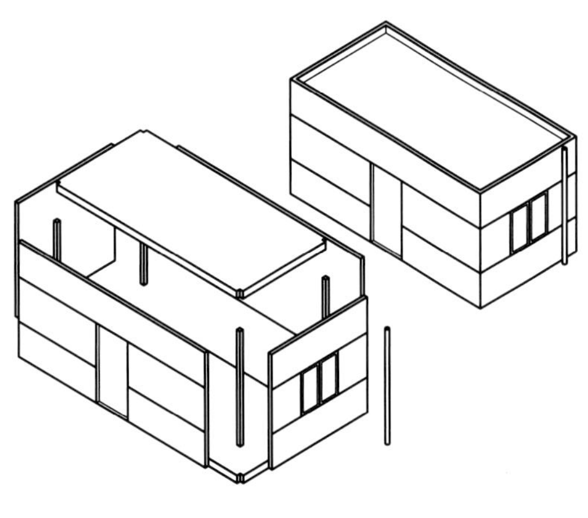

10

Design of a container module
Container systems closely follow the principles of lightweight construction. The design is derived from the construction of shipping containers and motor vehicles.

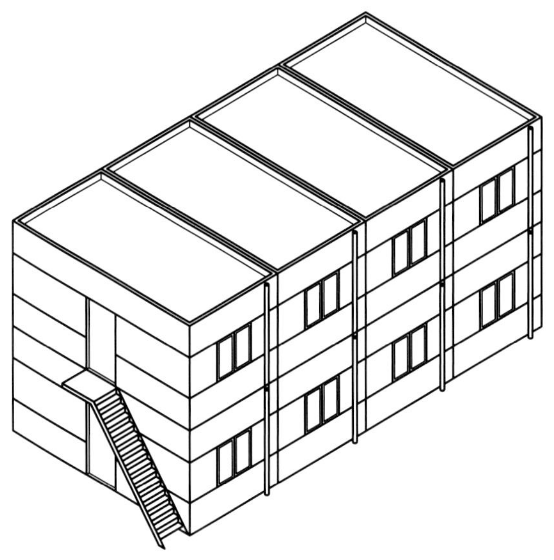

11

Container complex
Container modules can be brought together to form large building complexes.

Single-storey

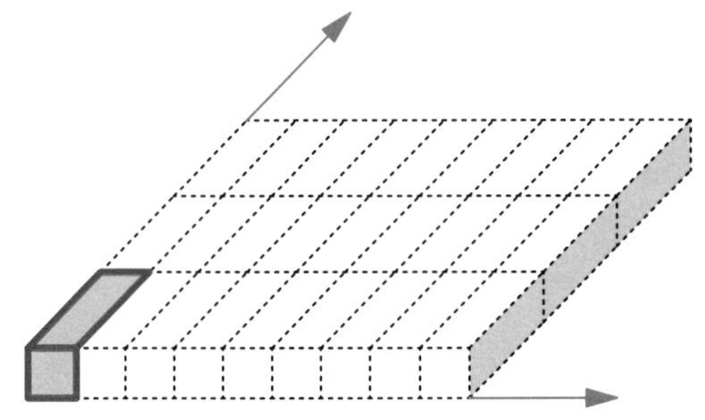

The containers can be added to one another in rows or set up singly. This arrangement can produce rooms of any size.

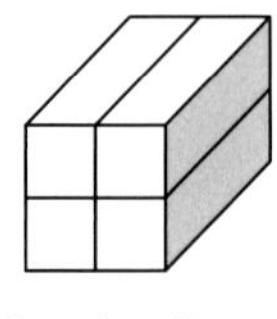

2 × 1 × 2

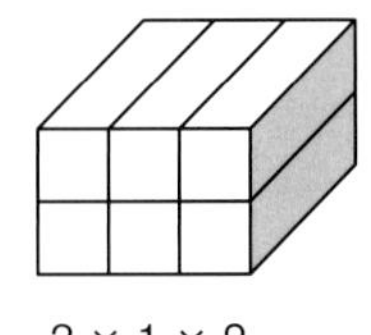

3 × 1 × 2

Any number of two-storey container modules can be added to one another in rows or set up singly. However, the stiffened external walls cannot be removed (max. room size is therefore 3 × 1 containers). The stiffened walls are shown by dashed lines, the internal space is open.

2 × 1

3 × 1

Two-storey

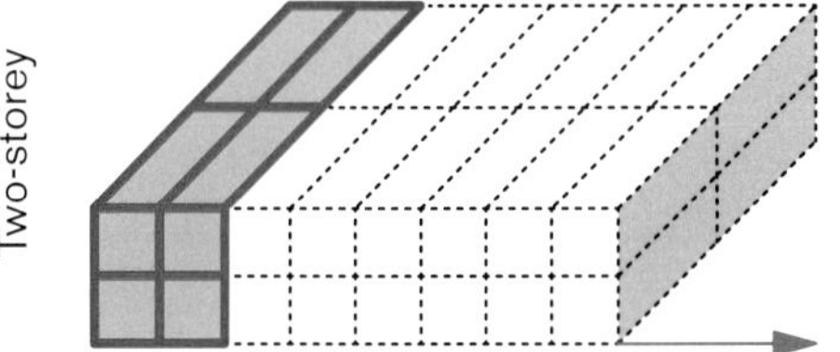

Multi-row container modules (number of longitudinal sides ≥ 2).
The system can be extended in the longitudinal direction from a minimum size of 2 × 2 × 2 containers. This arrangement can produce rooms of any size.

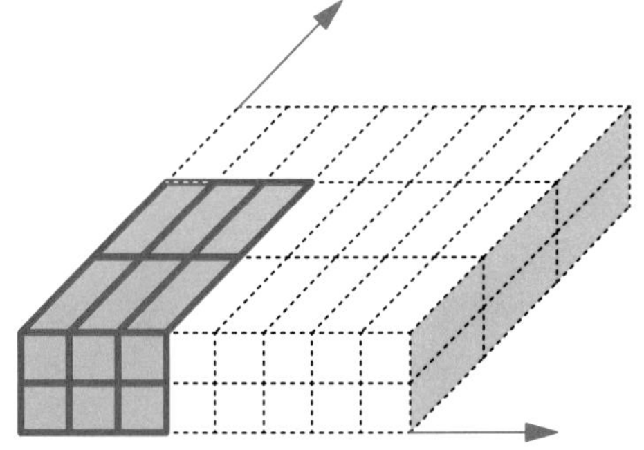

The system can be extended in any direction from a minimum size of 3 × 2 × 2. This arrangement can produce rooms of any size.

Three-storey

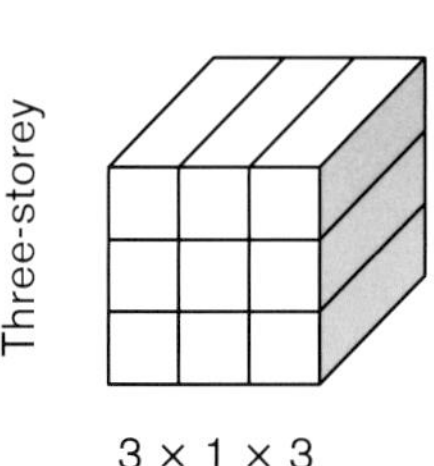

3 × 1 × 3

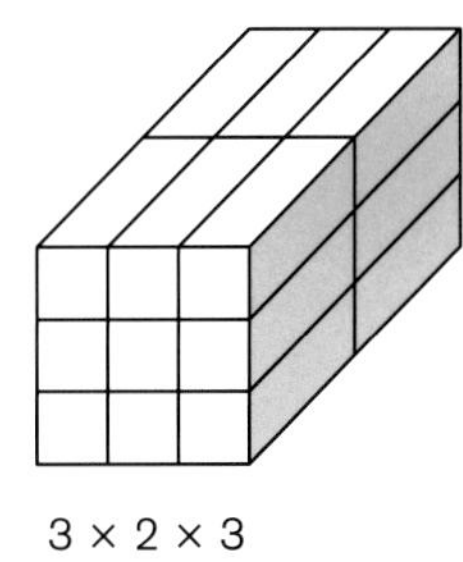

3 × 2 × 3

Any number of the three-storey container modules shown here can be added to one another in rows or set up singly. However, the stiffened external walls cannot be removed (max. room size is therefore 3 × 2 containers).
The stiffened walls are shown by dashed lines, the internal space is open.

3 × 1

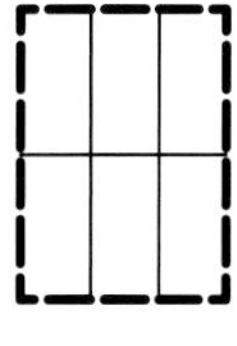

max. 3 × 2

12

Various options for container modules and stacking arrangements
Various combinations of container modules in one- to three-storey complexes.

tions by exposed diagonal bracing. The costs of a 1.50 m deep foundation, the additional structural measures and time-consuming intensive supervision pushed this tower structure financially into the cost zone of a conventional high-rise building.

13

Tower for Freitag lab AG, Zurich, Spillmann Echsle Architekten, 2006
The tower of container modules serves as offices and showroom. Preused containers were recycled for the tower structure.

Flexible modular systems

A good example, which will be discussed below, is a system that has proved very popular in the Netherlands (14). It has been available since 2000 as a semi-permanent or permanent building system, mainly for offices and schools.

Design

The modules are built on a standard, self-supporting, basic steel-frame structure (15). The steel frame is made up of a floor panel, four corner supports and a roof panel (16). The floor panel consists of a cement screed subfloor cast on a trapezoidal profiled steel sheet soffit, which is welded into a rectangular steel frame. The roof panel is similarly constructed, but with a weather-resistant bitumen sheet waterproofing membrane and an internally piped rainwater drainage system. Every module has a roof, even though the module may end up hidden within the heart of the building. The roof is necessary to provide weather protection during temporary outdoor storage before the modules are transported to the site.

14

Friesland Foods Building, Deventer, the Netherlands, 2007
Example of a flexible modular system.

The customer's choice of interior fittings and façades can be added to the basic module. Lightweight construction must also be used here, on the same principle as the basic structure. Gypsum plasterboard is used for the internal walls. The façades consist of aluminium window systems in a wall constructed from lightweight building boards, mineral fibre insulation and aluminium sheet cladding. After the modules have been fitted together on site, diagonal struts are installed on the façade or inside the modules to stiffen the building (17). Components such as stairs and lifts are installed conventionally on site to complete the building (18). The module dimensions were chosen to allow transport without special permission and to avoid travelling time or road width restrictions affecting the movement of lorries on public roads. Unlike flat-pack systems, where the walls can be transported in a compact package along with the roof panels, the modules in this system can only be transported in the completed state. The modules, complete with fitted out interior, are therefore low-weight/large-volume loads. The basic structure of the brick-shaped modules, with their strictly defined dimensions and design, considerably reduces the scope for architectural creativity with respect to overall shape, façade type and interior fit-out. However, within the limits imposed by the module and the lightweight construction principle, there is still room for customisation. The innovation of this system lies in the manufacture of the modules, where extensive prefabrication achieves highly

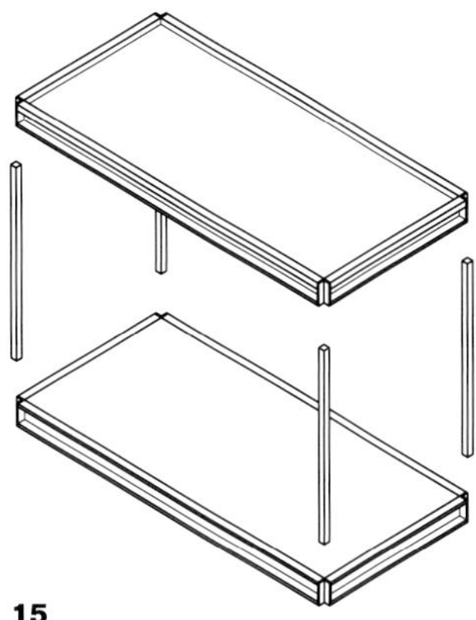

15

Design of modules
The modules are built on a standard basic structure, which consists of a self-supporting steel frame construction.

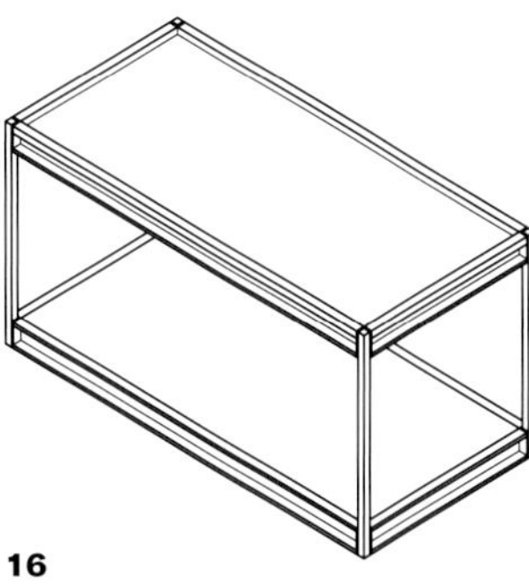

16

Construction of modules
The steel frame is made up of a floor panel, four corner supports and a roof panel.

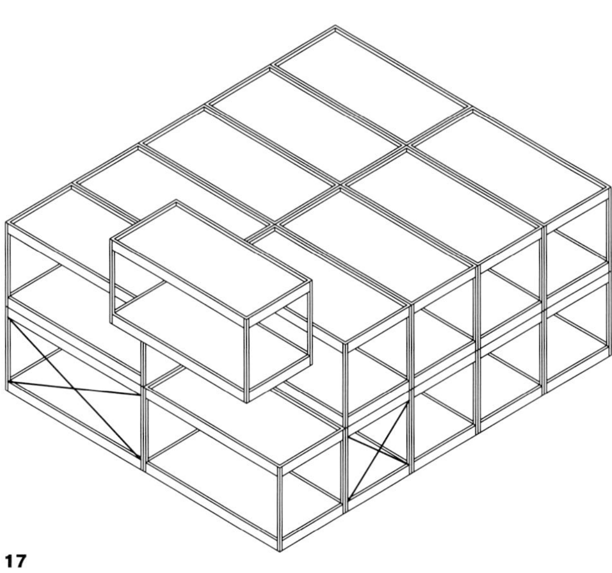

17

Design of modular buildings
After the modules have been fitted together on site, diagonal struts are installed on the façade or inside the modules to stiffen the building.

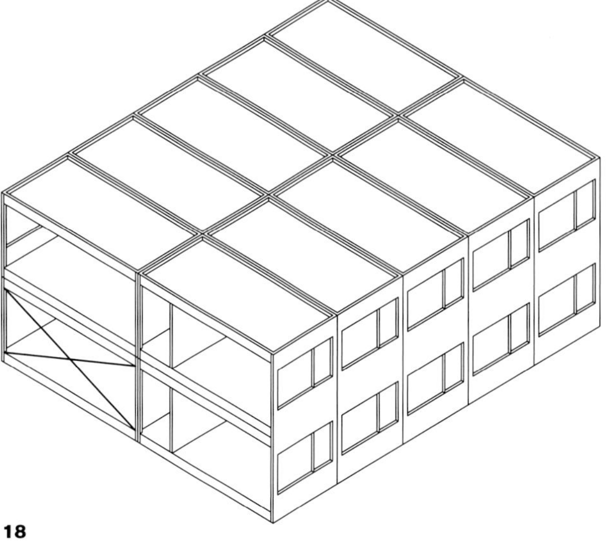

18

Modular building
Components such as stairs and lifts are installed conventionally on site to complete the building.

efficient production. The degree of prefabrication in conjunction with ease of transport and rapid erection on site greatly shorten the design and construction process and emit less pollutants, noise and dirt.

In Switzerland a modular system has been developed that uses wood, a local natural material. Walls, floors and roofs are fabricated on an assembly line using wood panel construction techniques, including the final wall surface. Window openings can be created up to a module width of 12 m. In addition to standard leasing solutions, wooden modular systems have been developed from the standard modules for hospitals, schools and offices, often in cooperation with architects (19).

19

The adapto modular system by ERNE AG Holzbau, Laufenburg, Switzerland, Kündig Bickel Architekten, 2000
Wooden modular systems have been developed from the standard modules for hospitals, schools and offices, often in cooperation with architects. This pavilion was completed as a kindergarten in 2000 and subsequently adapted for use as a meeting and presentation room.

Steel skeleton construction

Steel skeleton construction is used frequently in system building. Steel is a good material for system building because it combines high strength with low volume and weight, making it cost-effective to transport. Steel components can be prefabricated very precisely. The greatest disadvantage of steel construction in comparison with concrete is the extra work required to provide adequate fire resistance and to manufacture the roof and wall surfaces. The standardisation of steel profiles and sections means every steel structure is a form of system building. Every element of a loadbearing steel structure is designed in detail, then fabricated in the factory and assembled on site, like the parts of a modular system. Determinant for the suitability of a system is the extent of agreement of the modular grid with the overall building system grid. The various building systems differ greatly in this respect. The systems developed by Büro Haller were modularised down to the smallest detail to ensure that the buildings were as customisable in their configuration as possible, while other providers, such as Goldbeck, developed a more cost-effective mixed system involving concrete slabs for its Gobaplan system, which limited modularisation to the structural frame and the façade. The lower intensity of modularisation keeps the system more flexible, but also moves it closer to conventional building methods.

Midi system

The Midi system was developed in 1970 by the architect Fritz Haller from Solothurn, Switzerland, in cooperation with Swiss steel fabricators USM of Münsingen. The system was based on a steel skeleton and was intended for multi-storey buildings with a high proportion of building technical services installations, such as schools or administration offices (20), and was later extended to form the design tool Armilla, a digital layout system for services infrastructure in buildings. The system is still being further developed and adapted by the team today. The idea behind the system is to create buildings capable of being modified quickly and without destructive intervention to allow a change of use. All system components are designed to be easily removed at a later stage and reused on other sites, without being damaged or causing damage. A Midi building can therefore be extended in any direction or taken down, quickly and inexpensively (21). Midi is an integrated building system composed of six basic parts: loadbearing, floor, roof, internal wall, façade and installation systems.

These building components are developed as prototype models, which are used to finetune their modularity. Armilla is a general installation model for media supply and disposal systems

20

SBB Training Centre, Löwenberg, Murten, Switzerland, Haller Bauen und Forschen, 1982
Skeleton frame of a Midi system building.

21

Structural frame and completed building, SBB Training Centre, Löwenberg
All system components are designed to be able to be removed again after installation and reused at other locations.

22

Beam system with building services lines, SBB Training Centre, Löwenberg
The geometric arrangement of the beams meets the structural engineering requirements and allows efficient passage for the technical services lines in the plane of the beams.

and their networks. It is a computer-assisted toolkit for the design and operation of reusable buildings with a high building services installation content.

The steel building system has two basic components: circular steel columns as vertical support members and steel trussed beams as the horizontal distribution members. The vertical columns were made continuous and laterally restrained in order to avoid having to use disruptive stiffening elements. The trussed beams are placed in pairs and are made up of a combination of Warren and Vierendeel type truss members. The geometric arrangement of the beams meets the structural engineering requirements and allows efficient passage for the technical services lines in the plane of the beams (22). With a construction depth of 100 cm, the double trussed beam construction was selected because it allows pipes, cables and ducts to pass from the plane of the beams into the internal walls, even if the services lines coincide with the building grid. To allow the loadbearing system to be capable of being extended or reduced in size in any direction, the end and internal columns are identically dimensioned, as are the end and internal beams. The screed is precast on a trapezoidal profiled steel panel supported on the trusses and acts as the floor construction and the firestop between storeys. The truss soffits are concealed in offices and educational rooms with suspended panel ceilings or in corridors with an open metal grillage ceiling. The services installations are freely accessible for subsequent alterations or additions. The changeable arrangement is determined by the loadbearing system (23) and the Armilla model services installations design tool. Other systems, such as façades and internal fittings are specially coordinated on a project-by-project basis.

A square structural grid of 2.40 × 2.40 m was selected to permit the building to be extended or reduced in any direction at a later date. The fit-out grid of 1.20 × 1.20 m is based on the structural grid (24). It is superimposed congruently on the structural grid. The selection of a fit-out grid based on a multiple of 60 cm is beneficial to compatibility with other fit-out systems, such as double floors, kitchen or sanitary systems, which are frequently installed on a 60 cm grid. No storey height is stipulated.

In the context of building form, the Midi system is flexible to a limited extent, as the square grid and the orthogonal structure are predetermined, and therefore the architecture is also based on an orthogonal design. This applies to the external and internal forms. Of course these rules contain much scope for variations.

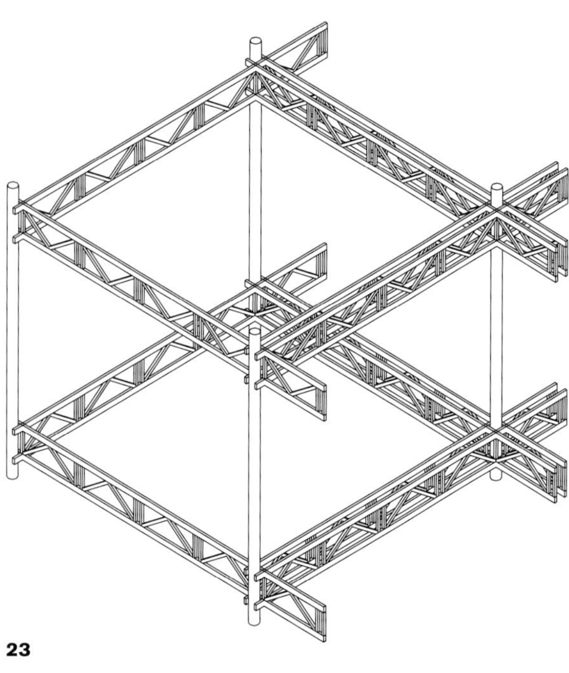

23

Midi loadbearing system
The steel building system has two basic components: circular steel columns as vertical support members and steel lattice beams as horizontal distribution members.

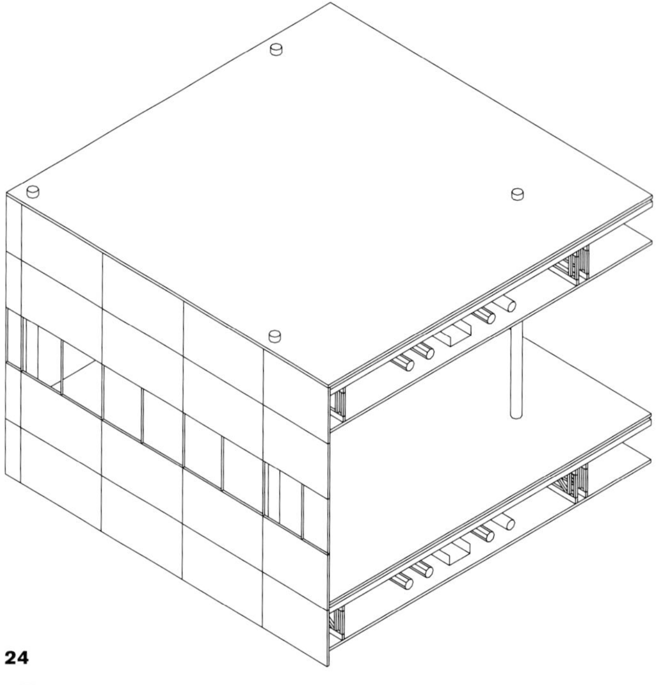

24

Midi system
A square structural grid of 2.40 × 2.40 m was selected to permit the building to be extended or reduced in any direction at a later date. The fit-out grid of 1.20 × 1.20 m is based on the structural grid.

The deep floor construction, through which the building services lines are distributed, allows for a great deal of variation in their layout, irrespective of where the vertical services shafts are located. The façade, which is spatially and structurally independent of the loadbearing frame, can be relatively freely designed. The real distinguishing feature of this system however is the flexibility for later alterations and conversions. The time required to remove or install internal walls, ceilings and installations is often only a few hours, and the work can be carried out by in-house personnel. Superfluous wall or ceiling elements can be placed into storage for future use.

The attention to detail and complexity of the system is remarkable. The idea of creating a building system capable of being varied on all levels, from structural frame to building services, has been fully and consistently realised. The system reflects all the experience Büro Haller has gained in the course of its research activities and the completion of built system applications since 1961. Because of its complexity, all the advantages and options offered by the functionality of the system only reveal themselves to the building designer after intensive involvement with its structure and methodology. Although the comparatively high construction cost has meant that this system has not been widely adopted, these construction costs become less significant when viewed in relation to those of operating a building and the costs of altering it later for changes of use. Clients have only recently started to consider life cycle costs in their investment plans. The future opportunities for this building system are likely to arise from its approach of component recycling and reuse, which scores well in life cycle analyses, and from its suitability for computer applications.

The Midi system, together with the Armilla installation model, has been implemented four times on projects by Büro Haller since 1970. Fritz Haller describes all the previous buildings as prototypes, in which the latest state of research was applied in practice.

One approach to the revitalisation of former industrial sites is illustrated in the Kraanspoor project developed by Amsterdam architects OTH – Ontwerpgroep Trude Hooykaas (25). An old crane track in a former shipyard on the north bank of the IJ river in Amsterdam provided the basis for a new office building. The structural grid of the office building uses a module of 23 m, which corresponds with the support layout of the crane track, and is subdivided into three bays of 7.67 m and superimposed on the old 270 × 8.70 m runway. The main loadbearing structure

25

Kraanspoor Office Building, Amsterdam, OTH – Ontwerpgroep Trude Hooykaas, 2007
An old crane track in a former shipyard on the north bank of the IJ river in Amsterdam provided the basis for an office building. The new building's structural grid is based on the existing column spacing of 23 m.

consists of HEB-300 and HEB-240 steel column sections welded to a Slimline deck system made up of IPE-270 I-sections and a concrete slab.

The special feature of the Slimline floor system (26) is that the building services distribution takes place within the floor construction, which contributes to a slight reduction of the storey height. Kraanspoor's lightweight steel structure is enveloped with a double-skin façade in the form of an internal room-high timber-glass façade and an external skin of sensor-controlled horizontal glass lamellae. The façade cavity can support foot traffic and serves as a room climate buffer. The building technical services system uses harbour water for concrete core activation and works with natural ventilation.

Mixed concrete-steel skeleton construction

Systems of this type cannot be reduced to generally applicable sizes, as each company likes to develop its own standards. A good example is the German office building system, Goldbeck, which is interesting because of its commercial success. Based on a core structure of a mixed concrete-steel skeleton structure, the building is effectively predesigned with a high proportion of standard details, which are used in all buildings of the same type. The repetition of critical construction features in the load-bearing structure and façade makes it possible to optimise the construction process and design with certainty of outcome. Goldbeck provides further confidence that deadlines will be met and budgets not exceeded by manufacturing the structural frame and façade, the most important of the prefabricated compo-

26

Slimline floor system

This floor system provides for the building services distribution to take place within the floor construction. (The photo shows the floor in the exhibition building for Bosch Siemens Homeproducts in Hoofddorp, the Netherlands; design: Mc Donough & Partners with KOW Architekten.)

27

Industry Park, Gobaplan system, Design Department Goldbeck, Langenfeld near Düsseldorf, Germany, 2006

Based on a core structure of a mixed concrete-steel skeleton structure, the Gobaplan building is effectively predesigned with a high proportion of standard details, which are used in all buildings of the same type.

nents, in the same factory. The Gobaplan system was developed in 1982 and is suitable a wide range of commercial property applications (27).

At the heart of the system is a structural steel skeleton made from I-sections and precast concrete floor elements (28). The steel beams are placed in a grid of 2.50 × 5 m or 2.50 × 7.50 m. This arrangement results in easily transportable reinforced concrete slabs with a maximum size of 2.50 × 7.50 m. The façade columns are positioned on a 2.50 m grid, but larger openings of up to 7.50 m are possible. The window spandrels are constructed with precast reinforced concrete units. They form the fastening points for the façade. The grid system for the beams is built on a multiple of the fit-out grid of 1.25 m. It is therefore compatible with the fit-out system, which is based on the German brickwork grid and its basic module of 12.5 cm. Drywalling, for example, has a basic grid of 62.5 cm. The loadbearing steel profiles are clad with plasterboard to provide them with the required fire resistance. The ceiling is terminated with a suspended ceiling, which hides the building services distribution ducts and pipework.

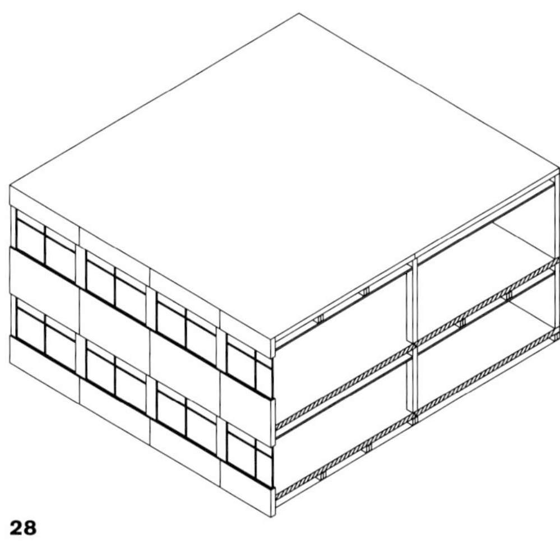

28

Gobaplan structural system
At the heart of the building system is a structural steel skeleton made from I-sections and precast concrete floor elements.

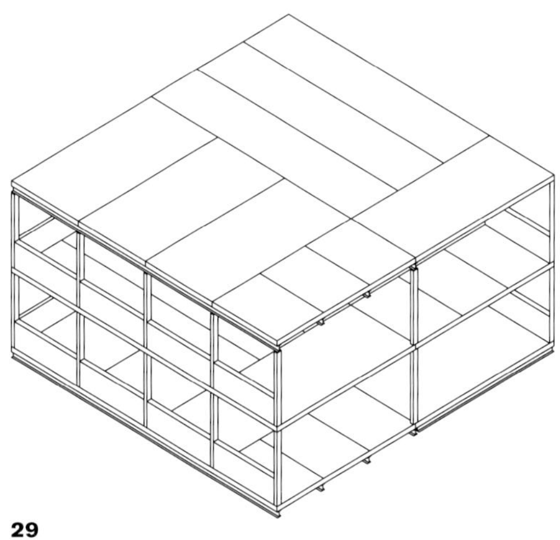

29

Gobaplan system
The system provides a ribbon window for the façade, which interrupts the façade columns spaced at 2.50 m centres.

30

Goldbeck showroom with 1:1 building models
Various versions of 1:1 building models are on show as marketing aids.

Gobaplan allows the architect a little flexibility and variability in the design of the building within the system. The external shape of the building is based on the orthogonal 1.25 × 2.50 m grid. The system provides a ribbon window that interrupts façade columns at 2.50 m centres (29). Within this construction the architect is allowed options in his choice of materials and window arrangement (30). Other façade variants are possible, but they are built conventionally and are not part of the building system. The structural design of the steel frame permits long spans, which results in fewer intermediate columns and much more flexibility for the interior fit-out. Depending on the choice of internal fit-out system, there are system solutions that permit later modifications and alterations to be made cost-effectively. Building services distribution behind the suspended ceiling retains the flexibility of office floor layouts. The sanitary cores depend on the position of the utilities shafts. Building services innovations, such as concrete core activation, cannot be incorporated because of the suspended ceilings.

The Lloyd's Building in London is an icon of prefabrication (31). Built between 1979–1986 by Richard Rogers, the offices are an example of a highly specific formulation of a modularised building. The complex consists of three main towers and three service towers around a central rectangular space. The outstanding feature of this insurance building, in addition to its striking

31

Lloyd's Building, London, Richard Rogers, 1986
The outstanding feature of this insurance building is the design of the vertical circulation elements and the services supply and disposal systems on the external façade.

appearance, is the design of the vertical circulation elements and the services supply and disposal systems on the external façade. This permits maximum flexibility in the division of the floor areas and eases the task of maintenance of the short-lived components of the building services systems.

Over the next few years, Rogers focused the approach of his office consistently around prefabrication and was able to enormously increase the efficiency of his practice by developing a continuously growing in-house details catalogue. Not surprisingly in 2004, with an annual turnover per employed architect of £ 248,936, he was ranked third in the list of British architects.

Concrete skeleton construction

The advantages of concrete compared with steel structures are their superior behaviour in fire, better sound insulation and the fact that the surfaces of the structural members can also be the building's finished surfaces. Disadvantages of concrete systems in office construction up to now have been the wide supports and deep beams of the loadbearing structure, which interfere with internal finishings and the efficient layout of building services, as well as the lower strength of concrete compared with steel. Over the years, systems have been developed, such as the CD20 Building System (32, 33), that are free of wide supports and deep ceiling beams. The use of prestressed concrete expands the structural possibilities of these systems, so that they

32

Building carcass for an office complex with CD20 Building System
A concrete skeleton system producing a flat, uninterrupted ceiling, which consists of columns and prestressed concrete floor slabs without downstand beams.

33

Carcass for an industrial building using the DW Systembau structural system
The concrete skeleton system consists of a combination of columns and floor beams. The roof and the walls are terminated with concrete slabs or other envelope materials (mostly sandwich constructions).

are capable of competing with steel building systems in the above respects.

The building for the municipal energy and water company in Buchs, Switzerland, was designed by Ballmoos Krucker Architekten and is completely prefabricated apart from the stairwell cores, which were constructed with in-situ concrete (34). The loadbearing façade columns are manufactured as composite elements, and the cantilever canopies are built directly into the main structure. The building focuses on the tectonics of the prefabricated components; the impression the building creates is one of confidence in a system-built building. The topographical integration of the building and the architecture of the façade and canopies communicates the subtle differences and the characteristic expression, while emplacing the difference between system building and architect-planned prefabrication.

34

Office building for the municipal energy and water company, Buchs, Switzerland, Ballmoos Krucker Architekten, 2004
The topographical integration of the building and its architectural grace can be attributed to architect-planned prefabrication.

Platform systems

The Individual Building Platform is an integrated platform system for office buildings (35) based on a concrete skeleton. The system was developed in 2007 by the Faculty of Architecture of TU Delft in cooperation with German and Dutch companies. It is designed to be capable of later adaption for other uses. The system is based on the platform strategy, a method of manufacture borrowed from the automobile industry, in which individual variants are built on the same serially produced platform. The components of a platform were selected to ensure that with the greatest possible number of specified system components, a minimal influence would be exercised on the architecture. The platform consists of four subsystems: building structure system (36), façade system (37), services system (38) and internal fit-out system (39).

An overall system is being developed based on the platform system for individual applications. In addition to the platform components, project-specific components are being developed for integration into the platform construction and design processes. This will allow just-in-time installation to be used throughout the site.

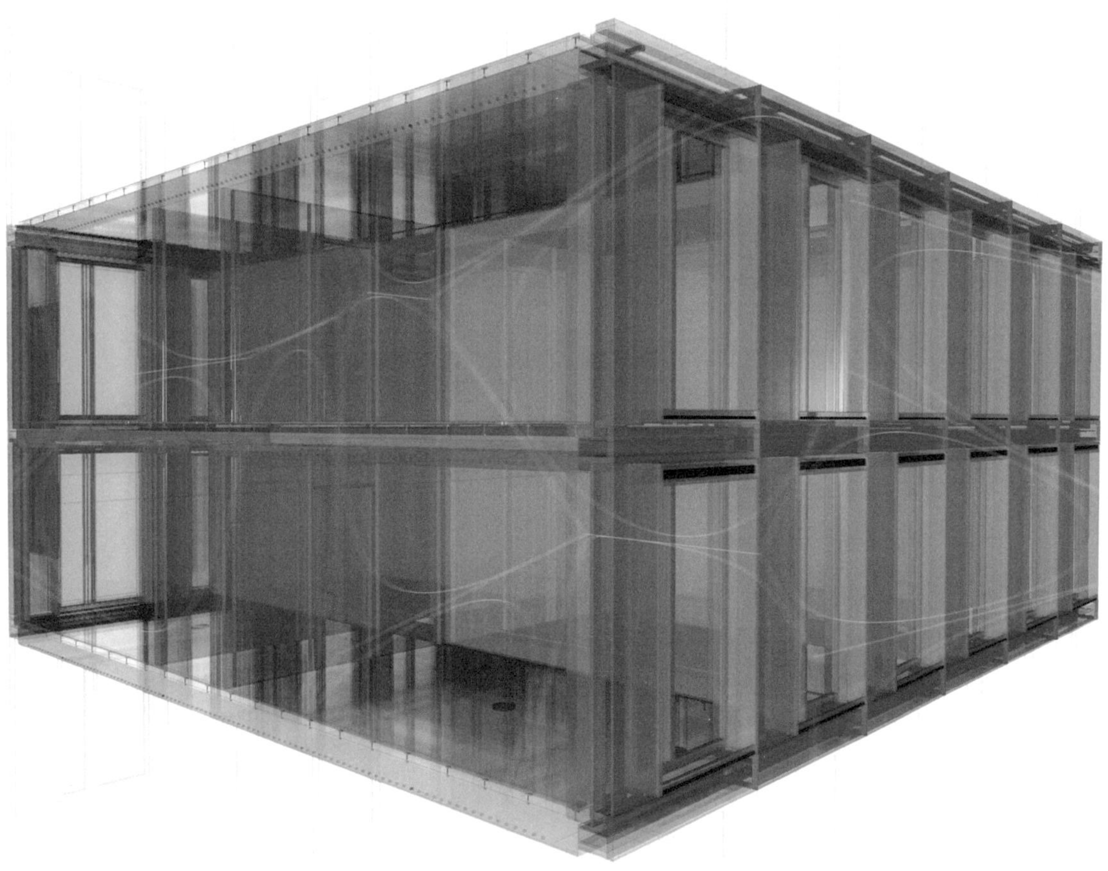

35

3D simulation of the overall system of the Individual Building Platform, TU Delft, the Netherlands, 2007
This system for office buildings is based on the platform strategy, a method of manufacture borrowed from the automobile industry, in which individual variants are built on the same serially produced platform.

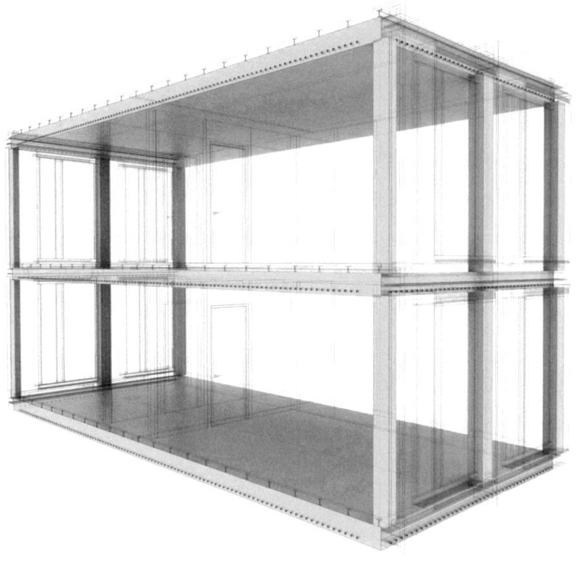

36

Individual Building Platform: building structure system
The building structure system consists of precast prestressed concrete slabs and reinforced concrete columns, which are connected to one another with a form of steel coupling with no projections below the structural ceiling soffit.

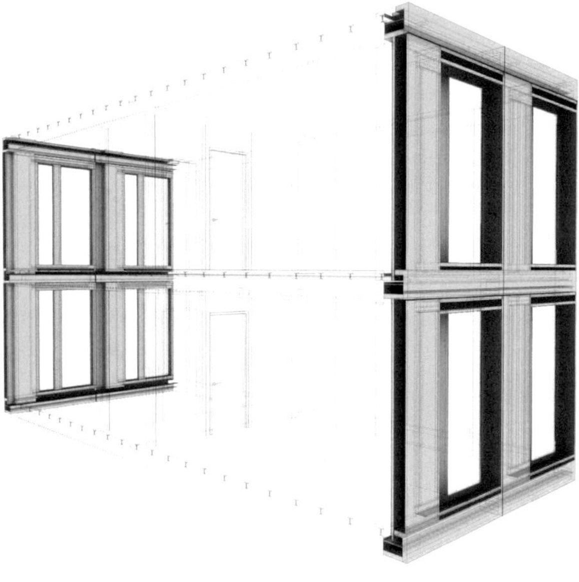

37

Individual Building Platform: façade system
The façade system was conceived as an element façade to allow the highest possible quality façade to be erected as quickly as possible.

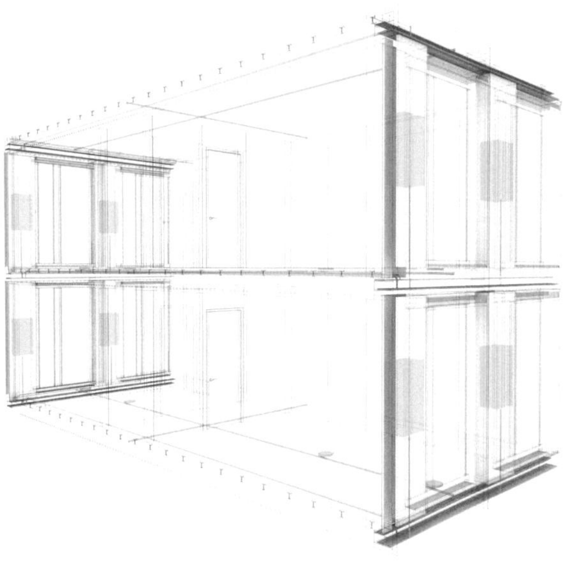

38

Individual Building Platform: building services system
Building services components are mainly located in the façade, and the façade interfaces to permit great flexibility inside the building.

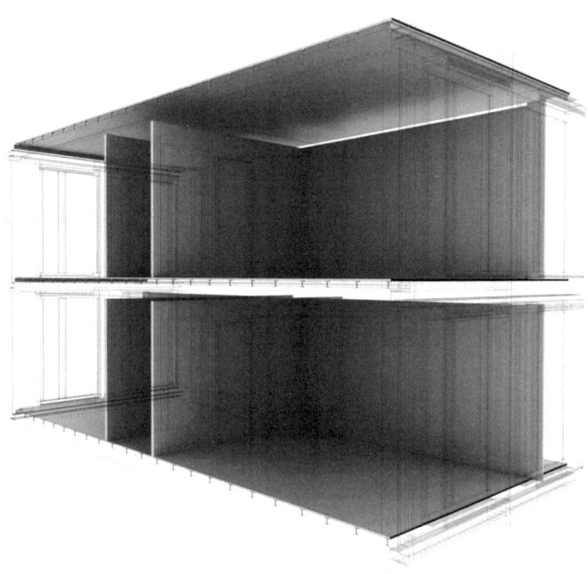

39

Individual Building Platform: internal fit-out system
The internal fit-out is completed with modular components to ensure an efficient predefined construction process inside the building.

The building structure system consists of precast prestressed concrete slabs and reinforced concrete columns, which are connected to one another with a form of steel coupling with no projections below the structural ceiling soffit. A void is created on top of the structural floor slab, which is part of a double-floor system. This void is available for the building technical services. The floor slabs can be part of a concrete core activation system. The façade is a modular services façade. It consists internally of aluminium window elements, building services elements and spandrel elements. Externally, it consists of double window or cladding elements in any selected material.
The fit-out systems for the internal finishings are chosen to coordinate with the overall system. The building services installations are defined in the design as individually modified modules. The services are distributed in the double-floor void and the building technical services façade module. The fit-out raster is flexible between the limits of 1.20 and 1.40 m. The size of the structural grid (40) can be varied between 3.60 and 4.20 m. There are no specified storey heights.

The platform's building structure system can create trapezoidal and circular buildings as well as orthogonal ones. Therefore the platform can cater to most commonly encountered building shapes. One-off parts of the building can be coordinated with the platform in the system. The cost-effective use of the systems is only possible with buildings in which the platform forms a considerable part. Flexibility of the internal fit-out is restricted in the case of façades with a relatively high proportion of columns and stiffening walls. The decentralised building technical services in the façade (41) and the double-floor construction open the way to flexible services planning. The system is currently still in the prototype phase and has not yet been used commercially.

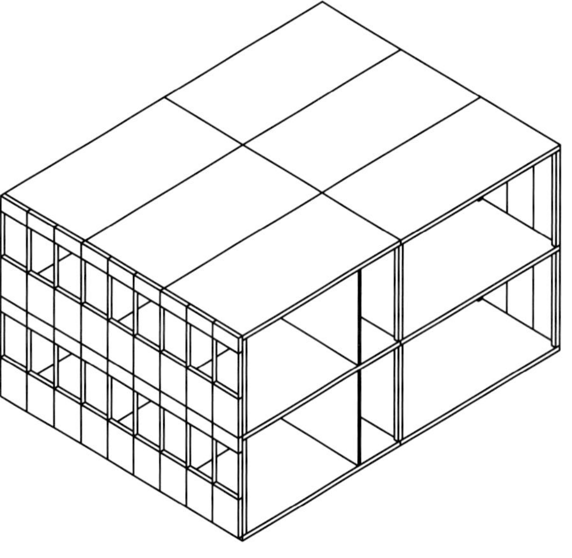

41

Individual Building Platform overall system
The façade is a modular component façade.

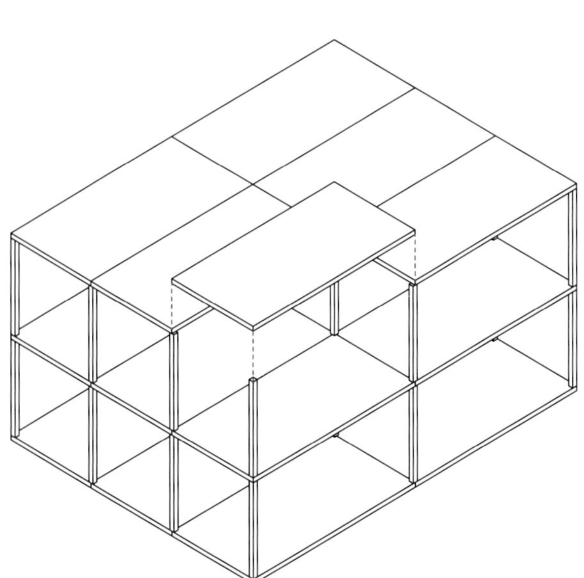

40

Individual Building Platform structural system
The size of the structural grid can be varied between 3.60 and 4.20 m. There are no specified storey heights.

Industrial buildings using precast concrete units

Industrial buildings cannot be considered as system buildings to the same extent as the office building systems discussed earlier in this chapter. An industrial building is created for a particular production process and designed to meet its specific needs. In the same way as high-rise buildings, the designs have so many repeating components that they can be viewed as customised system buildings with a high proportion of prefabrication. The designers can rely on system solutions to coordinate the various components, a job that is made much easier by the simple plan layout of industrial buildings. A system module consists of the following components: columns, beams, floors/ceilings, walls and façades (42–44). The purchaser is offered various versions of these components. All components can be varied in size and combined to suit specific needs.

A single-storey industrial building with metal façade elements as the external walls is taken as an example (45). The rectangular columns, which carry the horizontal forces acting on the façade, are bolted on to site-prepared foundations. The principal roof members are inclined I-section beams placed directly on the columns. Depending on spans, something like 6–9 m steel profiled roofing panels (46) or 9–12 m double T-slabs could be used for the roof panels.

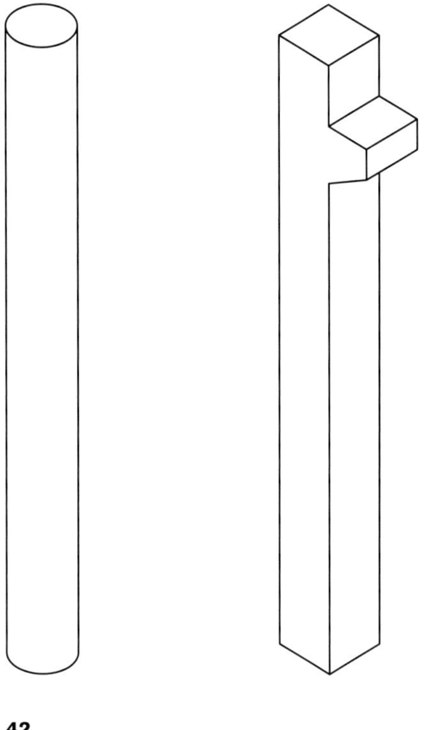

42

Concrete skeleton: columns
A system module consists of the following components: columns, beams, floors/ceilings, walls and façades.

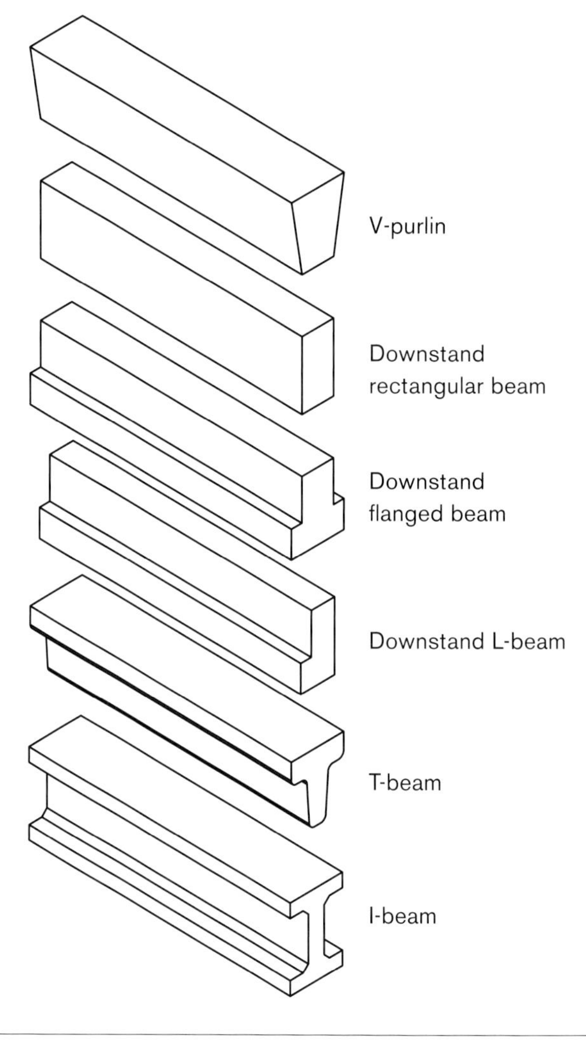

43

Concrete skeleton: beams
The purchaser is offered various versions of these components.

Market share for system-built buildings

The proportion of purely system-built buildings up to now used for commercial purposes in Europe in relation to the total built is rather small. In North America and Japan for example, prefabricated building construction is traditionally far more popular, but prefabrication must not be confused with system building, which is not very frequently used in these countries either. Only in the field of special buildings, such as temporary buildings or those simply built to fulfil a particular purpose, has the use of system buildings been accepted as the standard solution.

In the traditional building sector as well, there is worthwhile development potential in systems for permanent, complex and individual buildings, as can be seen in the rising success of a few specific companies. This sector has been largely ignored for years by major international construction companies. With very few exceptions, most system buildings have been designed by medium-sized companies with relatively small budgets for research and development. Future-oriented systems, aspects of sustainability, cross-platform construction methods are currently

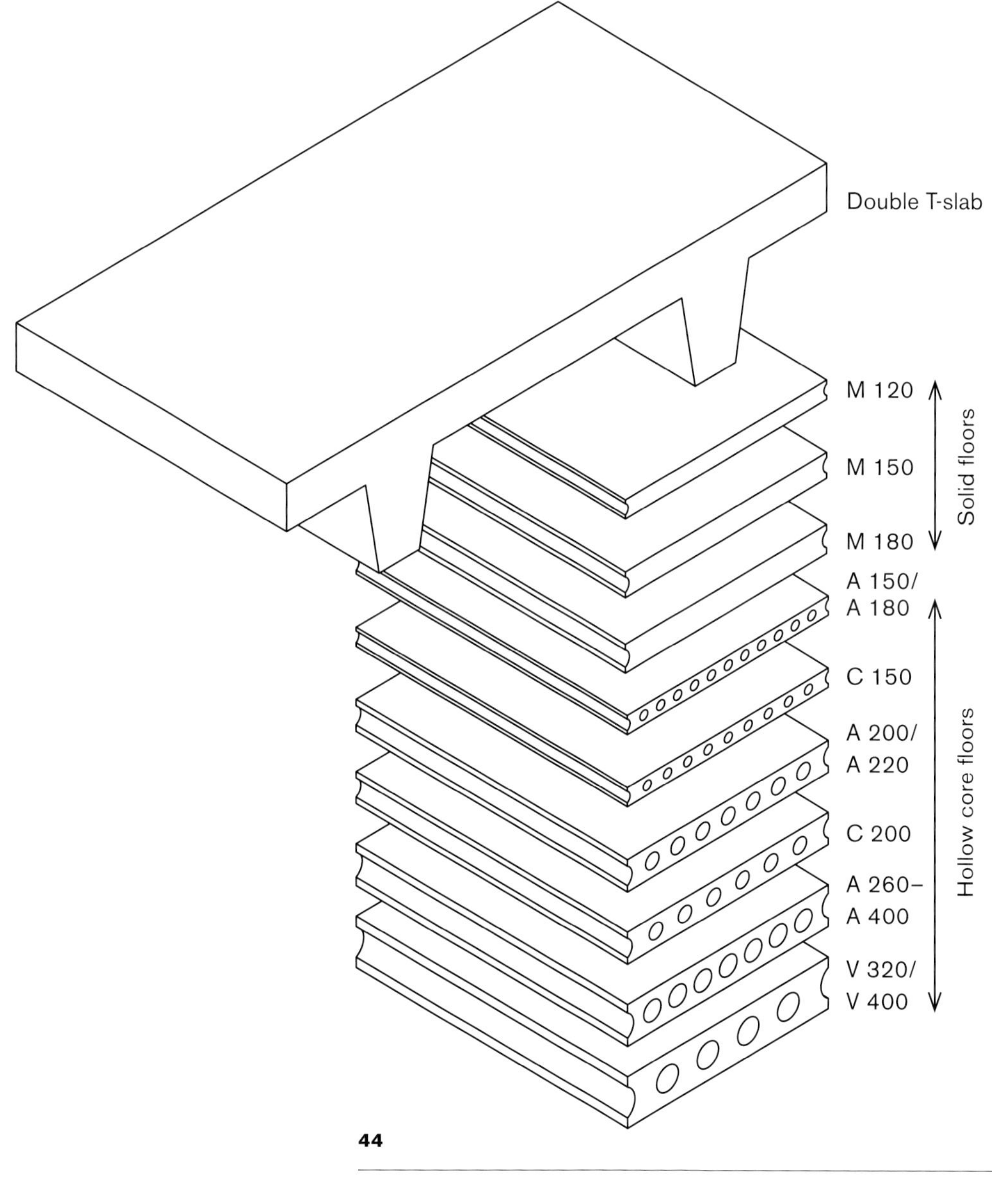

44

Concrete skeleton: floor/ceiling slabs
All components can be varied in size and combined to suit specific needs.

being developed in cooperation with universities of applied science. The Dutch Slimbouwen foundation was set up at the TU Eindhoven for this purpose by Jos Lichtenberg. This foundation links contractors, consulting engineers, architects and universities of applied science with the aim of promoting longer-term developments in the field of industrial, flexible and sustainable building. One of its objectives is to develop construction processes that will prolong the life cycle of a building. Adaptability and flexibility of the loadbearing structure is also addressed in the context of a long-term investment in which the needs of the future users are anticipated and planned for.

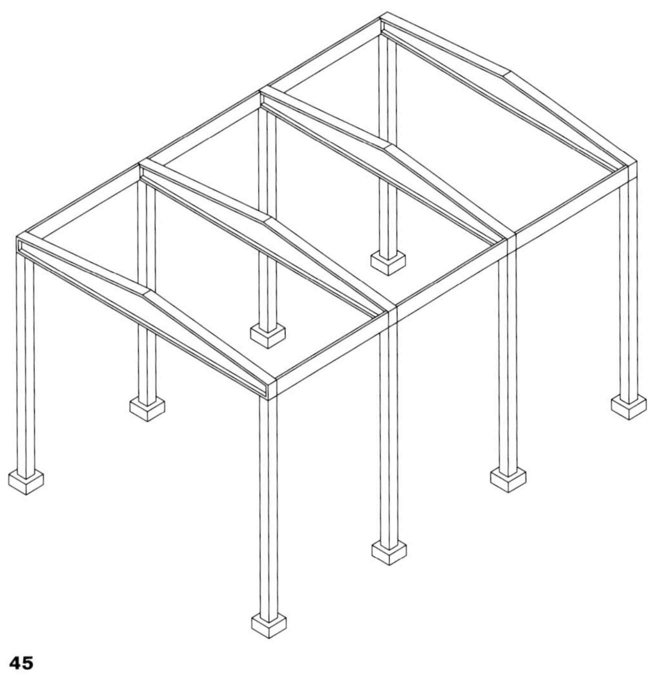

45

Structural members for a single-storey industrial building
This industrial building is an example of a concrete skeleton structure with a steel panel façade.

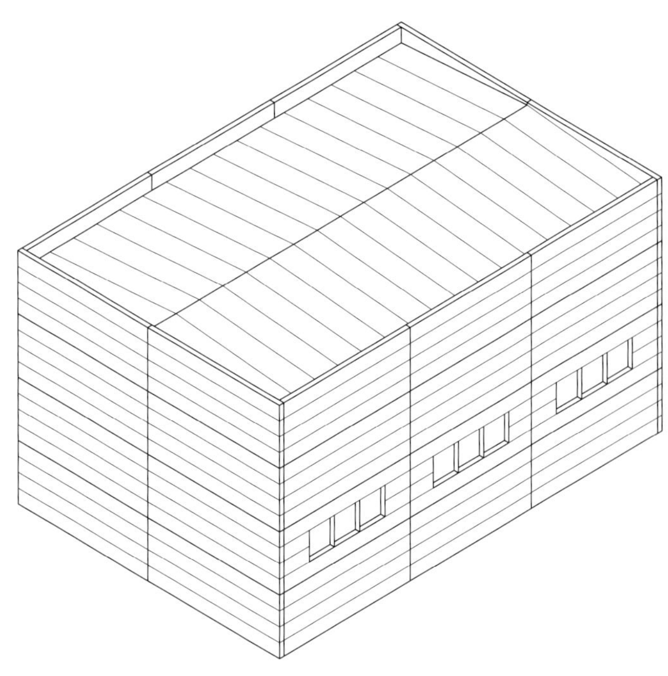

46

Single-storey industrial building system
Steel profiled sheets or precast concrete units can be used as the roof panels, depending on the spans.

5 | Processes

The process used to create a building is crucial for its later quality and manufacturing costs. A sign of a good production process is that it implements the customer's objectives efficiently from preliminary planning to the finished building, the production process can be divided into four phases: The planning and design, the production or prefabrication in the factory, the logistics of delivery to the construction site and the installation on site (1).

For production to be successful, process management (2) must achieve the required objectives in the following areas: cost management (low product costs, cost reliability for cost planning), time management (short design and construction phases, adherence to the planned time frame), quality management (adherence to quality standards). These objectives must be monitored and controlled throughout all phases.

The example of the automobile industry

The automobile industry is renowned for innovation within its manufacturing processes. Henry Ford, the founder of the Ford Motor Company in Detroit, revolutionised automobile manufacture with his introduction of the assembly line (3). Before then automobiles were hand-made, one-off items built in a cost-intensive and time-consuming process by skilled craftsmen. On the new assembly line, the workers did not go to the workpiece, instead the workpiece moved on the assembly line to the worker, who then had only a few simple steps in the overall process to complete time after time with the arrival of each vehicle (4). Using this method, Ford was able to more than halve the production time of his Model T from an initial 12.5 hours to 6. In 1909, the year following his introduction of assembly line production for the Model T, Ford manufactured 10,000 vehicles at a price of 950 dollars each. The profits were invested in the continuous improvement of his production techniques, which resulted in further efficiency gains and price reductions. Over the 19 years of production, he was able to cut the price to 280 dollars. By the time production stopped in 1927, Ford had sold 15 million of these cars in the USA alone. This production and sales record was only overtaken in 1972 by the VW Beetle.

Attempts were made during the 1920s with the manufacturing methods of the construction industry of modern architecture in Germany to transfer the success of Ford – the car for the masses – to living space. The primary goal, that of providing affordable homes for everyone, was not achieved even in Frankfurt am Main, where 15,000 residential units were built between

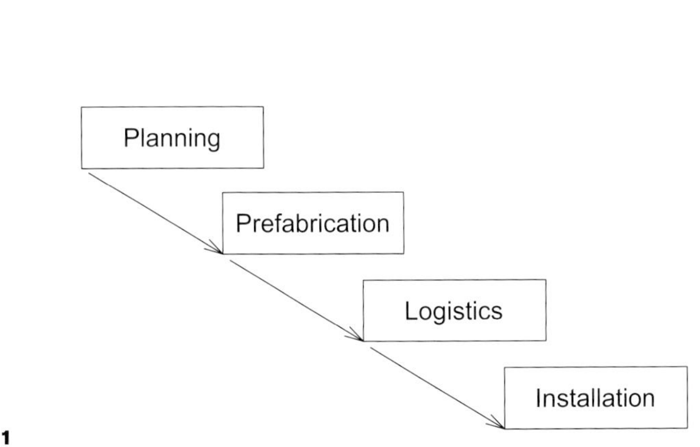

1

The four phases of the production process
Production or prefabrication in the factory follows planning and design; delivery to the construction site requires special logistics, and then installation takes place on site.

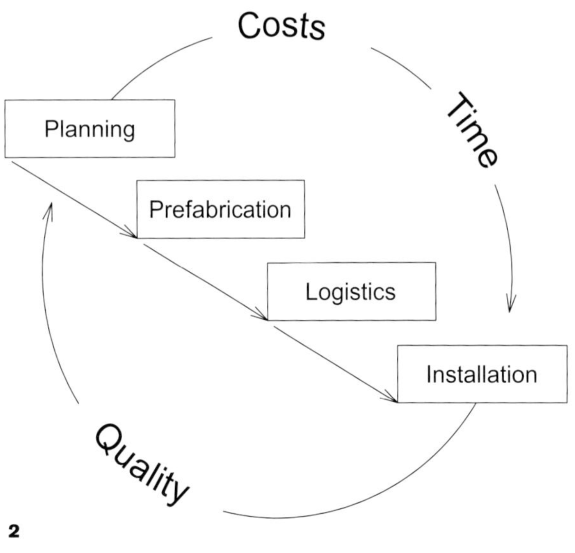

2

Cost and time management
The management of costs and time and the achievement of the required quality are the objectives for all process phases.

1926 and 1930 under the leadership of Ernst May. At this time, land prices were rising so rapidly, even during the planning phase, that the objective of creating a low-cost house for the masses was never achieved and the social ideas of modern architecture were never implemented. Many later attempts to mass-produce houses were unsuccessful for a variety of reasons.

Lean production

In the 1950s, Eiji Toyoda and Taichi Ohno started to further develop Henry Ford's production methods into the more flexible Toyota production system, also known as lean production. Eiji Toyoda had visited factories in the USA and discovered considerable potential for improvement in mass production. Adopting a different approach to mass production than at Ford, Toyota sought to make the whole production process efficient and

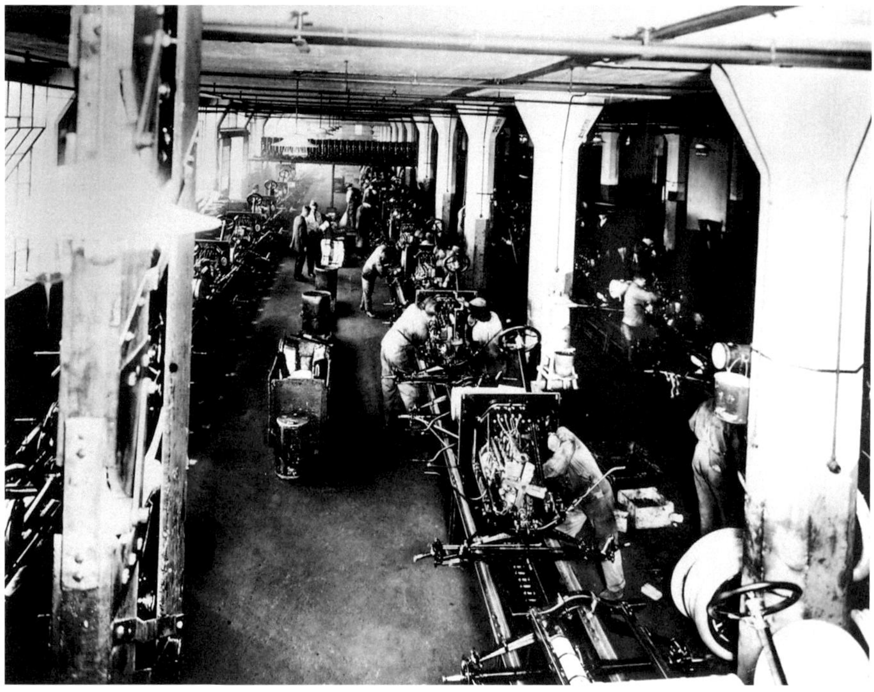

3

Assembly line production Ford Model T
With the introduction of assembly line production, the Ford Motor Company in Detroit revolutionised the automobile industry and transformed a manual, handcrafted production process into an industrial one.

4

Bringing together of chassis and bodywork on the Ford Model T
The components are preassembled on different floors and brought together to form the finished motor car.

flexible (5) while reducing the cycle time for each component. In essence, lean production avoids stock-keeping and transport. The production sequences are designed to be flexible and are based on a smooth work flow that can be adjusted to suit customer demand. To integrate deliveries from other companies into the assembly process, lean production prefers to have suppliers based as near as possible to the assembly plant. The workers participate directly and assume responsibilities in the quality management system. This process not only offers higher productivity and quality, it is considerably more flexible than mass production techniques in handling product diversity. Lean production allows different models to be manufactured on one assembly line. That today's stock exchanges regard Toyota as one of the most successful global car-making companies owes much to its logical implementation of this method of production.

Lean production's greater flexibility is also more suitable for the construction industry. It is successfully used by several system manufacturers, including Daiwa House Group from Japan and De Meeuw from the Netherlands.

However, the transfer of the technology from the automobile to the construction industry has its limits. An automobile is a mass product consisting of precisely engineered individual parts that are produced in large numbers and with very little variation. This does not apply to prefabricated buildings, where production numbers are much lower and components are too many and too varied to allow for customisation for the individual client.

System processes

Systems can be used to simplify complex design and construction processes. Their particular characteristic is that they are not permanently tied to one specific construction activity, but can be used as universal solutions. Systems may be classified as primary and secondary systems. Primary systems include all the components of a building and are normally oriented towards one usage type. Secondary systems are developed from single, closed processes, which are extracted from an overall building process and used as model solutions. As they are developed for a host of different applications, these model solutions can be viewed as optimised. The model solution process is continuously repeated and therefore is continuously redesigned and improved as a result of the experience gained in all its applications (6).

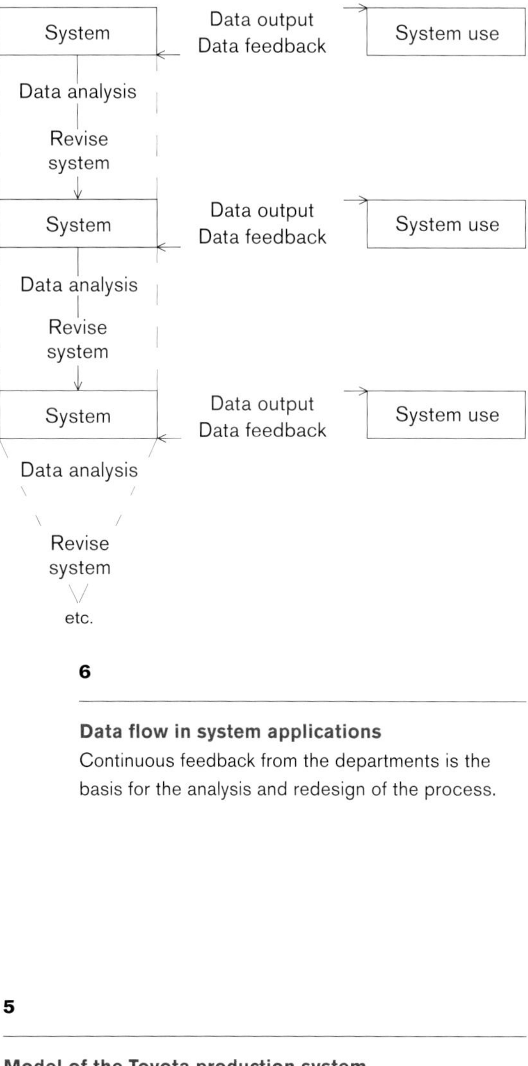

6

Data flow in system applications
Continuous feedback from the departments is the basis for the analysis and redesign of the process.

Best quality – lowest cost – shortest possible throughput times – highest safety – high workplace morale
Shortening of production time through elimination of non-viable elements

Just-in-Time

The right parts in the right quantities at the right time

- Cycle time
- Continuous flow
- Pull system
- Short re-equipping times
- Integrated logistics

People and teamwork

- Selection
- Decision making using the Ringi system
- Common goals
- Cross-working

Continuous improvement

Elimination of non-viable elements

- *Genchi genbutsu*
- 5W method (Five questions for finding out about why something happens)
- Awareness of waste
- Problem solving

Jidoka

Process-immanent quality in every working situation makes problems obvious

- Automatic production stop
- Self-controlled defect recognition
- Quality control in every working situation
- 5W method

Production levelling *(heijunka)*

Robust and standardised processes

Visual management

Philosophy of the Toyota method

5

Model of the Toyota production system
Lean production with the central idea of continuous improvement, which must embrace the complete manufacturing process and all the participants.

Design

Design is a process in which the form of the building, its construction method and sequence are determined and defined. Cost, time and quality objectives are determined and their sustainability improved. Decisions made at this stage can only be corrected in subsequent phases to a limited extent. Cost management is an example of the influence that design has on the whole of the building process. The ability to influence costs reduces considerably after the design phase (7).

Cost estimates and completion times can be precisely met only if the design team adequately considers the sequences of events and operations of the later production processes. Design has effects on the entire building process, from the initial concept to the details on site. As the design and construction processes are very closely interrelated and the initial design stages largely set the course for all subsequent actions, all the design participants, including if possible the contractors, should be brought together early in the life of the project to form an integrated design team.

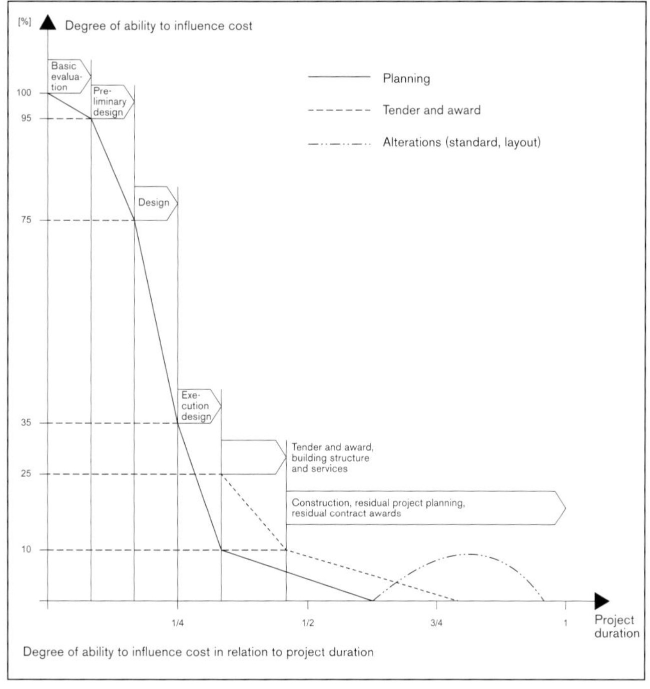

7

Ability to influence costs related to construction phase
All cost, time and quality objectives are determined during design. The ability to influence costs reduces considerably after the design phase.

Design systems

Design systems are the latest development in system building. As with construction systems, the idea is to transfer knowledge from industrial manufacturing into the building industry. They are developed by construction companies and universities of applied science. For about twenty years now, architects have been designing almost all their buildings on computer-aided design (CAD) systems. These systems allow design data in the form of CAD drawings to be used directly for the computer-controlled prefabrication of components in computer-aided manufacturing (CAM) processes. Closed CAD/CAM processes are frequently used in industry, but their application in construction processes has been much less common until recent times. Architects' methods of working are often still as remote from prefabrication processes as they were before the introduction of CAD. Design systems allow closed CAD/CAM processes to be introduced into building projects.

Design systems determine the construction process in a series of established iterative design steps. Construction processes, as defined in these systems, are individual construction processes that are not tied to particular companies, construction methods or products. Using these systems, architectural designs can be translated into project-specific construction systems. These systems have the advantage that they can cater for every architectural variant. Their disadvantage is that very little influence can be exerted on the costs, works programming or quality management of the eventual contractors during the subsequent construction phase, as the design systems have not been finetuned to specific companies.

Construction systems

Construction systems stand in contrast to design systems; one example is the modular building system (8), which was developed from constructional and logistical principles. With these systems, design is determined by the constructional and logistical requirements of production processes. The greatest difficulty is to produce individual architecture despite the design being based on a modular system and a standardised construction process. If a system is based on elements with fixed module sizes, it can only approximate the requirements of a specific design. The individual design is adjusted to suit the modular dimensions, which often involves significant changes. The advantage of these systems lies in the repetitious construction process, which generally falls under the sphere of influence of a contractor. It allows costs, works programme and quality to be centrally controlled and accurate estimates of these parameters to be made at the design stage.

Computer-aided design systems

Digitales Bauen was established in 1998 with the objective of transferring the experience and knowledge of many years of research at the Institute for Industrial Building Production (IFIB) at the University of Karlsruhe into construction practice. The institute's principal areas of research in the 1980s and 90s were the building component systems of Fritz Haller, and in the context of this book, the Midi building component system and the Armilla installation model. Concepts for the comprehensive and consistent computer-aided design, construction and operation of these buildings evolved from a number of research projects. A new design methodology developed in which individual architectural designs were systematically defined, disassembled into modules, which were then recombined in an integrative process and finished in detail. The basic principle from which Digitales Bauen derives its methodology is that every building contains some degree of repetition and therefore can be defined using a module specific to that building. The house is not a serially produced product, but its individual components take a serial form within the overall system of a building.

The design process follows the examples of CAD/CAM processes found in other industries. A building is defined in terms of recurrently applied project standards, which are translated in the design in ways that allow them to be manufactured from data on CAD drawings and specifications in prefabrication works as parts of a specified modular component. This means that specific component parts defined by the architectural requirements are developed for every design. Controlling this process requires a suitable project organisation and communications structure to integrate all specialist disciplines, such as building services and structural engineering, and in the ideal case, the contractors who will eventually produce the building, into the design process at the earliest possible stage. The entire process chain, from planning and design, through prefabrication, logistics and assembly right up to facility management, is digitally controlled from a dataset over the whole project timeline. This means that all the construction and operating data of the building are accessible at any time during the process through integrated computer and database systems.

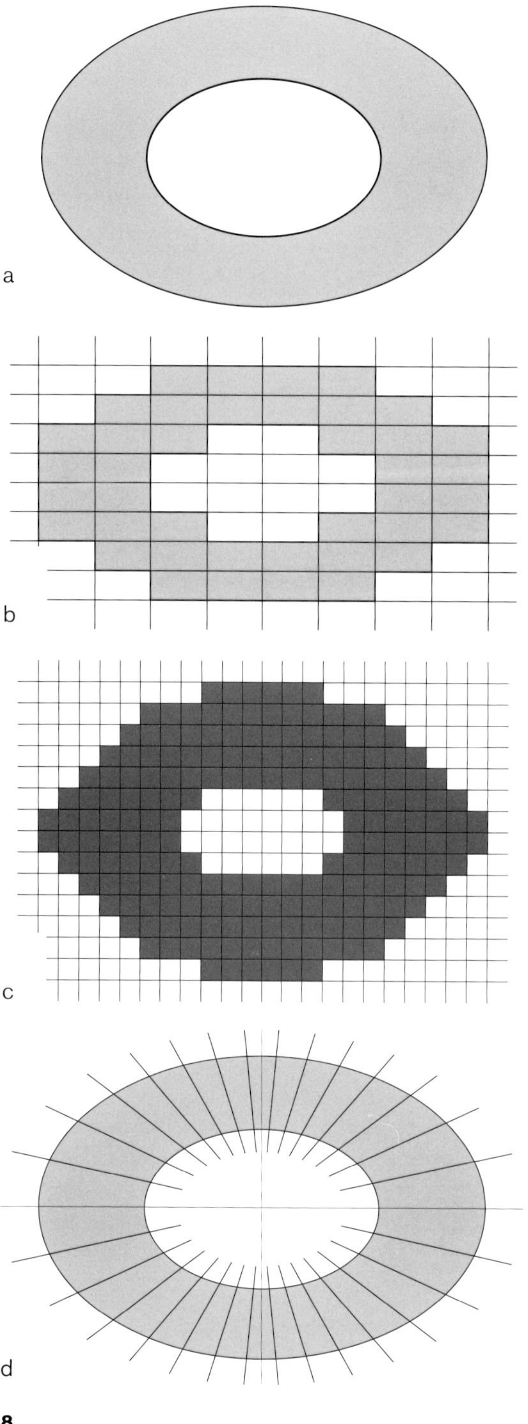

8

Operational principles of design and construction systems
The selection of a design or construction system is crucial to the exact implementation of the individual design and defines the degree of adjustment to the design necessary to fit in with the system.
a Individual requirements (design)
b Coarse grid of a modular building system (construction system)
c Finer grid of a modular component system (construction system)
d Individually adjusted modules in a design system

A similar strategy was followed in the design process for the Mercedes Benz Museum (9). A parametric CAD model was developed in an early stage of the design. The geometry was not described in terms of fixed values, but was dependent on further parameters, such as building services, structural engineering and building regulatory requirements. Mutual dependencies cause the effects of alterations of one parameter to be transferred to other project requirements and the adjacent areas to be reassessed. The design process required a cooperative working environment involving architects, engineers, mathematicians and computer scientists, in which problems could be solved using innovative and technically complex techniques. All project participants were able to work on the model at the same time, without having to spend time and waste bandwidth in transferring information over communications interfaces. The results could then be sent directly to the fabrication shops manufacturing the structural frame and façade members.

Construction process

Normally the assembly work on site is linked with the construction process. Little attention is paid to secondary construction processes, such as prefabrication and logistics, because most buildings are designed to be assembled and built on site. This is the case even though prefabricated semi-finished products, such as windows or precast filigran concrete floor panels, are also used on these sites. The three production phases of prefabrication, logistics and assembly are therefore present on all sites. The proportion of the on-site construction and system building processes taken up by the separate phases is different in each case.

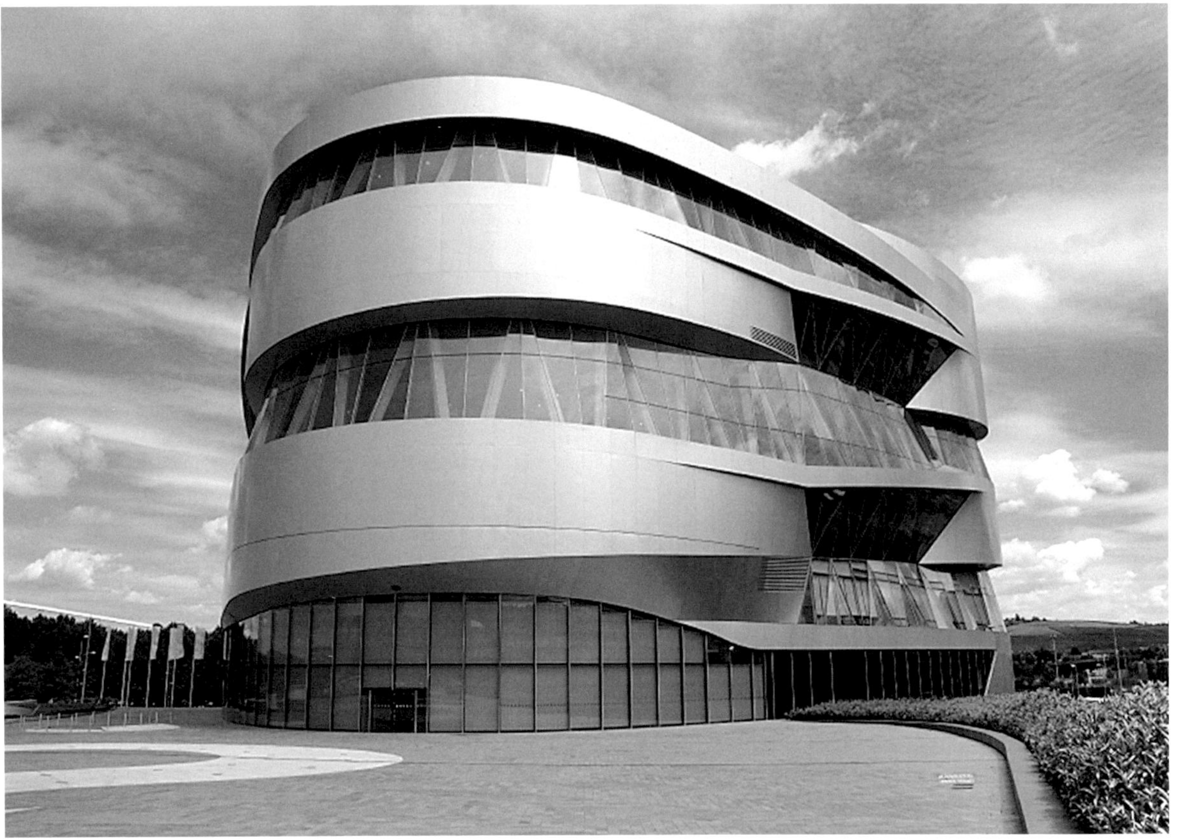

9

Mercedes Benz Museum, Stuttgart, UN Studio, 2006
The building resulted from an integrative and interlinked design process.

On-site construction

On-site construction predominates building production today. This means that, a very large proportion of production takes place on the construction site. Raw materials, semi-finished and prefabricated products are delivered to site, placed into temporary store and further processed by craftsmen. The construction processes for on-site methods of building are less specialised, and the investment in production is particularly low for the internal finishing works. The sizes of the companies involved in projects using these conventional building methods range from small firms to international concerns. Companies of many different sizes compete for the contracts as well. The intense pressure of competition leads in many cases to the on-site construction method appearing to be cheaper to the client than the prefabricated alternatives, in spite of its inefficient process structure. However, on-site construction also has crucial disadvantages. In many respects, the construction site is unsuitable as a place of production (10). It is spatially constricted. The different trades have to divide the unfinished space into working areas, with the risk that they will hinder one another in the cramped surroundings. At best they will be able to set up their tools, power and media supplies on a temporary basis. Storage is difficult, depending on the location of the site, and weather protection may be inadequate during certain phases of construction (11). The consequence is that on-site construction methods contain many hidden imponderables with respect to costs, the required labour hours and product quality.

10

The construction site as a place of production and storage

With the on-site construction method, the site is both a storage and production facility, which brings with it various disadvantages.

11

Skilled work on site

Raw materials, semi-finished and prefabricated products are delivered to site, placed into temporary store and further processed by skilled craftsmen.

Prefabrication

Many systems are developed with the aim of disaggregating the construction process as much as possible and shifting activities off the site and into the factory (12). For part of a building to be prefabricated, the design must be capable of being broken down into fabricated units suitable for factory production. These units, also known as components or modules, must be defined in terms of their weight, size and surface resilience so that they can be easily transported and handled during installation on site (14).

Prefabrication allows individual processes to be planned to take place spatially separate from one another and unhindered in specialist factories (13). In the factories there are no unfavourable weather conditions. Floor space can be laid out optimally for the production flow and use made of special equipment, such as assembly lines or automated systems. A further advantage of prefabrication in the factory is that the constant conditions allow each production step to be monitored more closely and meet higher-quality criteria. The investment costs for factory buildings and machinery are a disadvantage and must be taken into account in the prefabricated option.

12

Prefabrication of precast concrete units
Many systems are developed with the aim of disaggregating the construction process as much as possible and shifting activities off the site and into the factory.

13

Prefabrication of windows
For part of a building to be prefabricated, the design must be capable of being broken down into fabricated units suitable for factory production.

14

Prefabrication of steel girders
The prefabricated units, also known as components or modules, must be defined in terms of their weight, size and surface resilience so that they can be easily transported and handled during installation on site.

Logistics

Logistics are important for construction to proceed smoothly and efficiently. The required components or modules must be delivered exactly on time to avoid unnecessary standing time during installation or storage (15). Especially on system building sites, logistics have to be precisely coordinated with the rapid pace of the assembly of the components. The higher the degree of prefabrication, the greater the influence of logistics on the construction programme. Logistics is the tool for saving time and costs on site. The shorter construction time and lesser need for temporary storage space of system building processes give rise to considerable cost reductions for sites where site plant and facilities account for a high proportion of the total construction costs and on inner city sites in particular.

Installation on site

The basis of an efficient installation process is the precise planning of the work flow during installation. Every step and component must be considered in advance. The site must be laid out to allow unloading and handling of large parts or components with various options for loading and transport.

In an ideal construction process with a high degree of prefabrication, the work on site is reduced to the quick, just-in-time installation of finished components (16), which is carried out, in ideal circumstances, so simply that it can be performed by very little specialist labour (17). The complicated installation processes should be completed in the prefabrication stage. The risks presented by the changing outdoor conditions for on-site construction can be minimised by the shorter installation times. There are, of course, parts of the construction process that cannot normally be carried out by prefabrication. They are the first and last stages on site, which include the preparation of the site, foundations and the final interior finishings.

15

Delivery of precast concrete units
Logistics are important for construction to proceed smoothly. The components or modules must be delivered precisely on time to avoid unnecessary standing time or storage.

Quadrant Homes On-site system

A system does not necessarily have to involve a high degree of prefabrication. In some systems it may only be necessary to standardise and optimise the construction process on site. US-American housing company Quadrant Homes organises the on-site construction of detached houses in a way similar to prefabrication in the factory. The smooth work flow is achieved through erecting a large number of houses simultaneously and arranging the sequence of works for every house to match activities in the factory. This work flow is organised in the same way on every site and depends on an ever-increasing number of identically designed houses being built at the same time. The trades move like an inverse production line by following the production steps from house to house.

16

Assembly of the structural frame

For a construction process with a high proportion of prefabrication, the work on site shrinks to the rapidly executed, just-in-time installation of finished components.

17

Installation of internal walls

In an ideal construction process, the installation is so simple that it can be performed cost-effectively by unskilled labour.

Lean production for modular construction

The modular building system of De Meeuw, which is used in particular for offices, schools and hospitals (18), is an example of production process with a high proportion of prefabrication in accordance with the principles of lean production. The basic idea is to prefabricate modules of the maximum allowable size for transport by road. The transport of larger modules requires special permission, which would entail extra cost and have to take place at night. Up to 24 modules per day can be produced. The fabrication cycle is not fixed but adjusted to suit the requirements of the site. In accordance with the principles of lean production, the same production line could be used to fabricate different modular systems, for example MAX 21, Kombi 21 and Flexicom, all at the same time. Building services are installed by an external contractor in the same fabrication shop and integrated into overall finishings installation. The modules are taken from the factory's storage area and delivered just-in-time to the site, where they are installed in the building. The building is then finished by skilled tradesmen on site.

Lean production for component construction

Another builder of detached houses, the Daiwa House Group, works in accordance with lean production. Design takes place in a central design office from where the information is sent to the factory for prefabrication. In this system, instead of modules, the factory prefabricates components such as frames, roof trusses, façade panels, roof panels, ceiling and floor units. Here as well, the subcontractors are brought into the factory to assemble the prefabricated parts of the loadbearing structure or aluminium windows and make them ready for further stages of the overall building process. The installation of the various components takes place in parallel in the factory. The fabrication process is designed to allow prefabrication of individual variants, so that the proportion of standard buildings can be as low as 30 %. The factory prefabricates a complete house in only five hours. The prefabricated components are delivered to site and installed there by specially trained partner companies; internal fittings and domestic building services are installed by tradesmen to complete the house. Construction on site takes about three months.

a

b

d

e

Advantages and problems of systemised processes

The objective of every system development is the optimisation of the construction process. The area of systemisation depends on the initial circumstances and requirements. Systems are most successful when short design and construction times are required. Most systems have been developed to satisfy these requirements. A feature of many systems is the production of a more dependable and consistent quality of building compared with conventional construction methods. It continues to be difficult to produce a building using an optimised process more cheaply than using tradesmen and conventional construction methods. The prospect of continuously rising construction costs and, in some countries, a shortage of skilled labour increases the need in the future for an optimised construction process that will be more cost-efficient than conventional construction processes. The most important objective in the development of a system building process will be the ability to adapt the system to individual architectural designs. That this has not been adequately implemented in most construction systems in the past has been the main reason why system building has gained so little acceptance to date. This potential is only available from computer-aided design systems that are not limited to predetermined forms of construction and components.

c

f

18

The modular building system of De Meeuw is an example of a production process based on lean production principles

Prefabrication and installation take place in this order:

a Welding of the base plates; b Erection of the structural frame; c Fitting out with internal walls and façade; d Finished module; e Delivery; f Installation on site

6 | The Components: Systems, Modules and Elements

Systems and subsystems

This chapter discusses the division of building systems into levels of the construction or into individual components such as roof, façade, etc. or – alternatively viewed – according to work packages of the trades involved in the construction. Following on from this, the chapter discusses the degree of prefabrication of the construction and finally types of connections. These different ways of considering the construction are necessary to explain the different terms and building methods used.

A system is a structure of individual elements that form a whole. In the field of building this means that the individual components create the whole (1) – for example a house is put together from bricks (2). The development into more complex buildings, for example a skeleton structure with façade modules as an envelope and an interior formed with partition walls and technical services components, leads to a further division of the system into primary and secondary systems, and into modules and elements (3).

1

Natural stone masonry
Simple system of elements: natural stone masonry, constructed without mortar, is a complete system consisting of only one type of element.

2

Sagrada Familia, Barcelona, Antoni Gaudí, 1882–1926
The masonry is arranged to follow the flow of force, which results in the simplicity of the system composed of one type of element being retained even though the complexity of the geometry increases.

3

Conservatorium van Amsterdam, de Architekten Cie., 2008
A whole system consisting of several secondary systems (envelope, roof, etc.) with individual modules (façade) in turn consisting of individual elements (windows, etc.).

In a way similar to the procedure for dissection into different levels and associated elements, a system can also be represented as a geometric structure: the development of a construction system begins with the connecting nodes in space, i.e. the linking of several levels (4). In a second step, the individual elements of the construction are assembled and form the structural primary system. To define the space, these elements are overlaid with the secondary system of filling elements. The individual parts of the systems can be created from modules, which are made out of assembled elements or the elements themselves.

Alternatively the starting point can be the modules, which then become the assembled individual parts of a system (5). Here as well, the modules consist of individual elements. The result is a complex construction system from which a well-systematised and prefabricated structure can be created because it is based on complete modules or subsystems (6, 7).

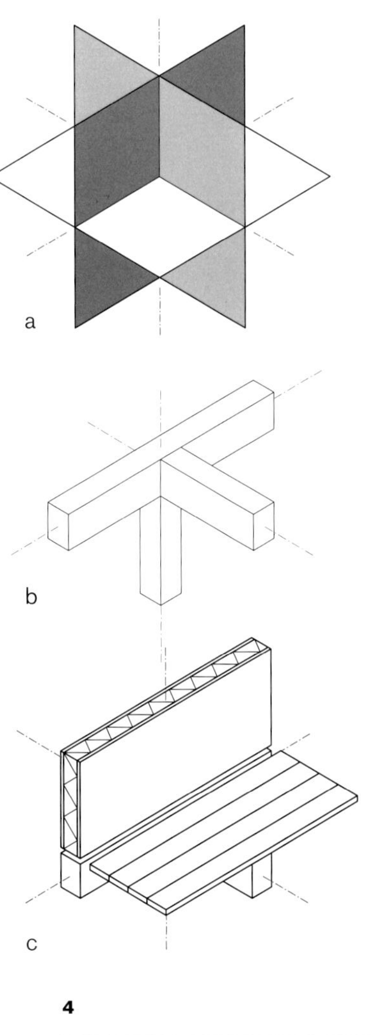

4

Developing the construction from the nodes
The geometry of the three planes defines a node in space (a), the primary system (b) forms the loadbearing structure, and the secondary system (c) acts as an envelope, in some cases with a loadbearing function.

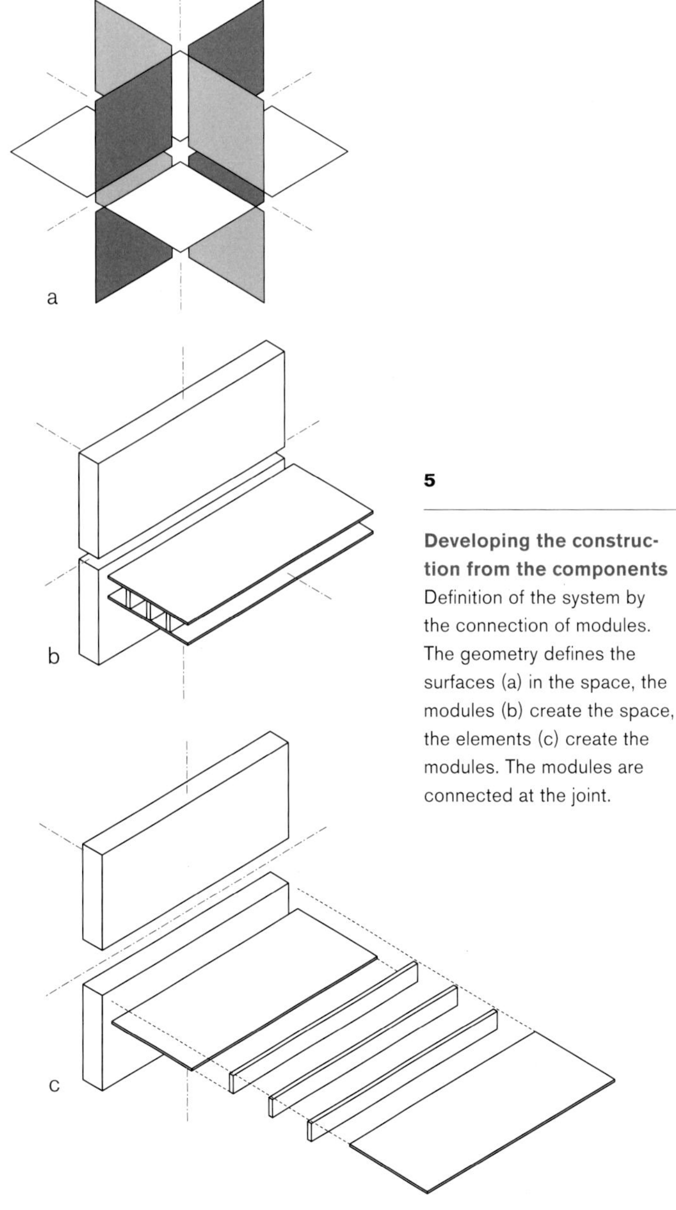

5

Developing the construction from the components
Definition of the system by the connection of modules. The geometry defines the surfaces (a) in the space, the modules (b) create the space, the elements (c) create the modules. The modules are connected at the joint.

Classification by levels of construction

Buildings can be subdivided into different construction levels:

The system, consisting of primary and secondary systems, describes the house as a whole, which in turn is made of modules such as walls, floors, etc. The modules consist of elements. The primary system usually represents the structural frame of a house, while the secondary system is the building envelope (8, 9).

Modules are: façade modules, windows, doors, stairs, roof systems, etc.

Elements are: bricks, window panes, window frames, roof beams, etc.

6

Post-and-beam construction in a façade
Detailed view of a façade construction made up of elements (e.g. post and double-glazing units). The assembly of the secondary system (façade) takes place completely on site.

7

Element façade in construction
Modular façade system in which the individual modules are prefabricated and installed on site with the aim of saving time.

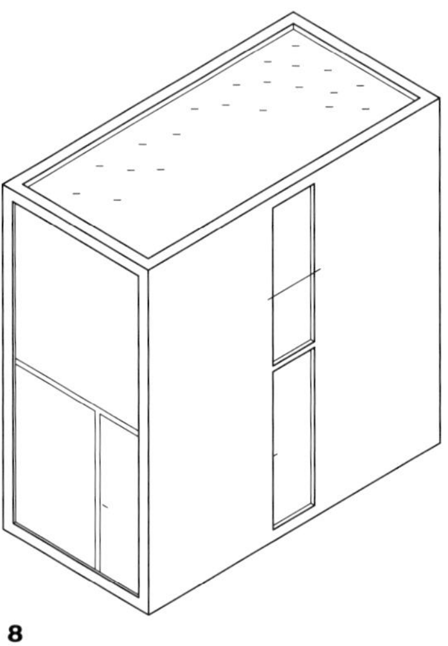

8

Primary system
Primary system, consisting of loadbearing walls, which in turn consist of secondary systems.

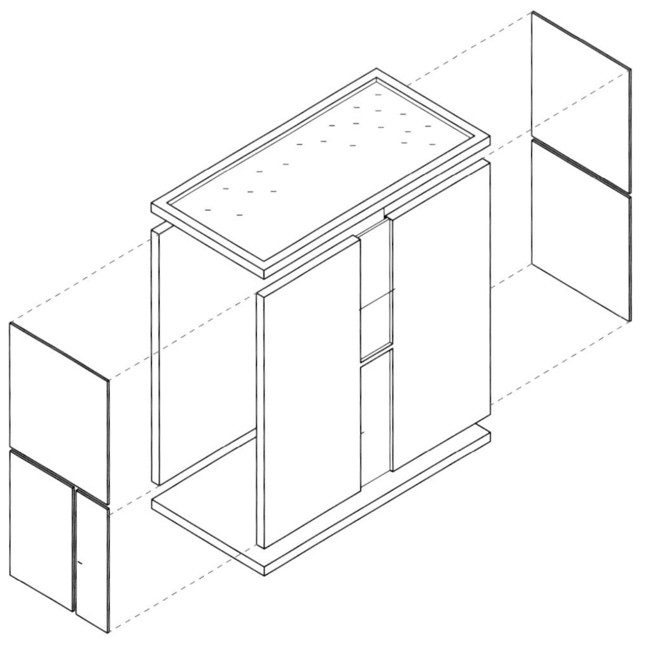

9

Secondary system
Secondary system, consisting of façades, walls, ceilings, roofs and floors.

This subdivision is hierarchical. Several elements can, for example, form a module and the assembled modules, the system.

Systems, whether at the level of the primary system or the secondary system, consist of modules. Distinguishing the modules of a building is simple, as long as the separation of functions is reflected in separate modules: a roof functions as weather protection, floor slabs carry the floor loads and separate the storeys. The same applies to further subsystems, such as partition walls, stairs or sanitary units, in as far as these are prefabricated as modules. The external walls, where they are loadbearing, can be a combination of loadbearing structure and building envelope. If these functions are separate, the parts can also be described as modules: the loadbearing structure on the one hand and the façade on the other (10–12).

Modules are assembled from elements. Creating modules, such as a floor structure, involves assembling individual elements, such as floor beams, boards, insulation, ceiling soffit and flooring. The same applies to roof structures, which are made out of structural members, insulation, roofing membrane and roof covering.

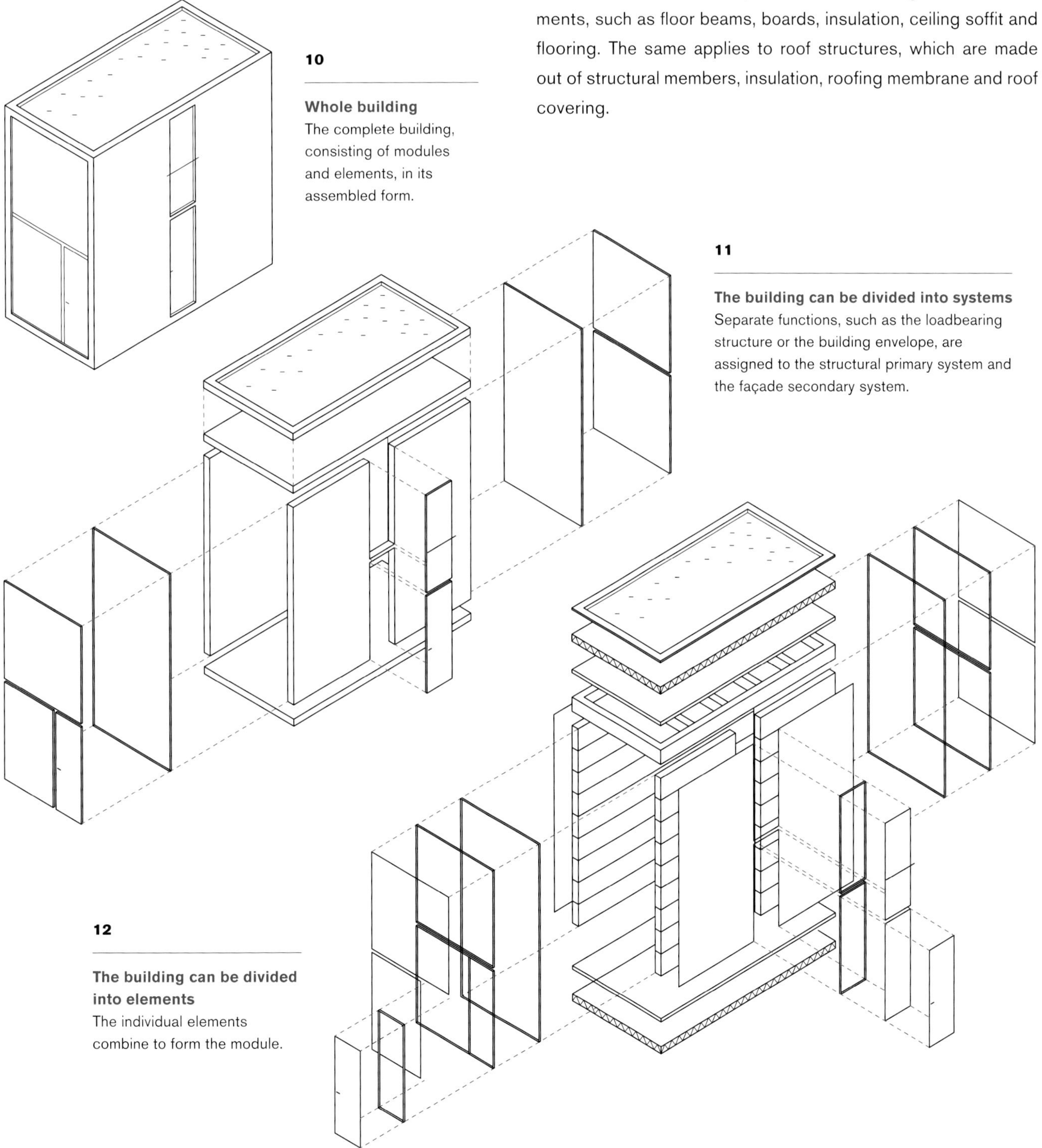

10

Whole building
The complete building, consisting of modules and elements, in its assembled form.

11

The building can be divided into systems
Separate functions, such as the loadbearing structure or the building envelope, are assigned to the structural primary system and the façade secondary system.

12

The building can be divided into elements
The individual elements combine to form the module.

Classification by construction trades

In addition to the division of a building according to levels of construction (system, module, element), buildings can also be subdivided according to work packages, i.e. logically amalgamated performance areas of the various trades. While the subdivision according to construction levels relates only to the unfinished building carcass with its comparatively large tolerances and the rather coarse, still imprecise method of building, here the work packages of finishings and building services are considered with necessary higher levels of precision.

This results in the following classifications:

- Loadbearing structure: the loadbearing parts of the building
- Envelope: the enveloping layer of the building, façade or in the case of a loadbearing façade, the outer skin of the wall
- Finishings: components of the finishings permanently connected to the building (not mobile furniture)
- Building services: technical equipment of the building, such as heating, ventilation, sanitary fittings, etc.

Normally the construction of a building begins with the loadbearing structure, which has the function of distributing the loads and to which the other parts are physically connected (13–15). Structures are differentiated between those which are purely loadbearing and those which also fulfil a space-defining role.

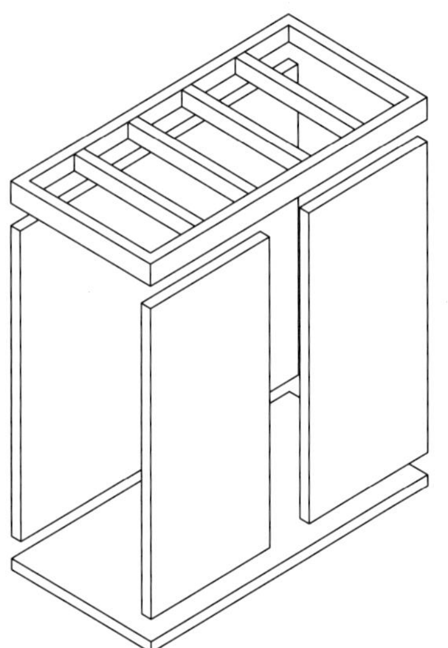

13

Loadbearing structure
Diagram of the loadbearing modules and elements of the building.

14

Loadbearing structure: skeleton construction
Example of a skeleton construction of reinforced concrete with internal reinforced concrete columns and ceiling slabs.

15

Loadbearing structure: external walls of reinforced concrete
Example of a loadbearing external wall of reinforced concrete. The insulation and weather protection are not yet installed.

The function of the envelope relates equally to the interior and the external protection of the building: the interior usually needs an inner surface that satisfies the requirements of the building use in terms of function and form. The external skin must repel moisture and temperature (16, 17). If the loadbearing structure also performs a space-defining function, the tasks of the envelope are either ensured solely by the selected material or by the presence of further layers.

The potential for the use of prefabrication is high in the construction of the façade. Preassembled elements can be installed, for example, in a post-and beam-façade with regular dimensions and identical or variable filling elements. Alternatively storey-high modules consisting of several preassembled elements can be brought to site and then simply installed in position. Transport logistics may allow the use of mega-units, the result of highly industrialised façade production, which are several building grid widths wide or may even form the complete building wall.

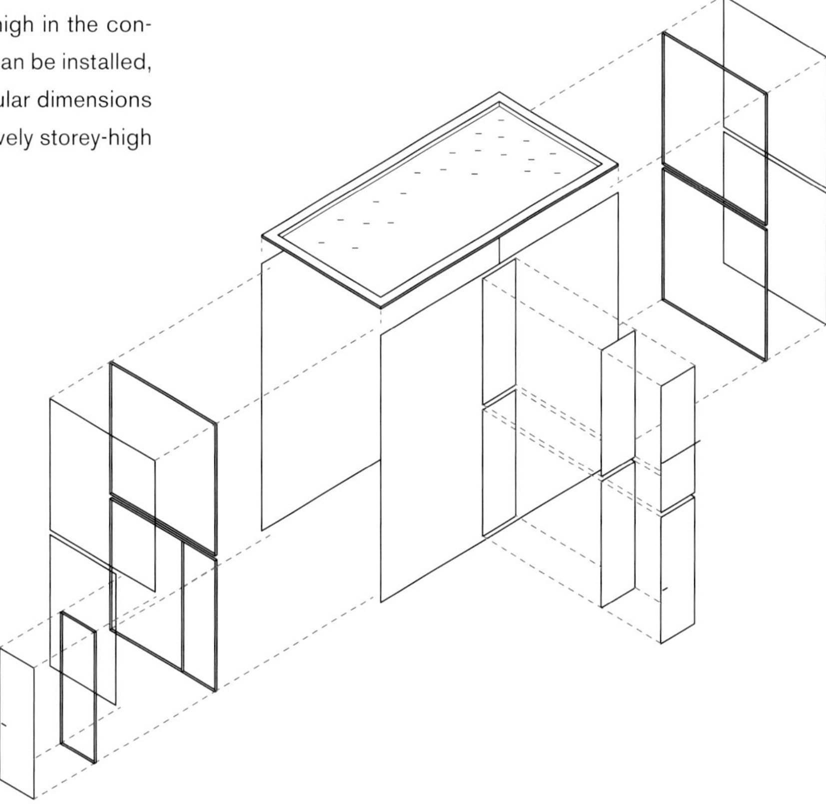

16

Envelope
Diagram of the modules and elements that surround the building and perform all the functions of the building envelope.

17

Example of an envelope
The loadbearing structure is clad with a modular façade, which fulfils all the functions of the envelope and is installed storey by storey.

Finishing elements include lightweight partition walls that do not perform a loadbearing function, finishing components (fixed furniture, etc.) and stairs that do not stiffen the whole system (18). Prefabricated sanitary units can also be considered as finishing elements.

Finishing works may involve a medium to high degree of prefabrication: lightweight partition walls for example, made from gypsum plasterboard stud walls consisting of prefabricated and easy-to-install elements (19). However, it must be noted that disassembly is only possible when some degree of destruction is involved. System partition walls on the other hand are fully prefabricated modules and therefore can be reused.

A high proportion of components in the field of building services are prefabricated: elements intended to be installed directly in the building are almost always prefabricated to factory-made quality (20, 21). This also applies to simplified connection techniques in which the use of couplers means that only the lengths of plain duct between the connections need to be measured and cut on site.

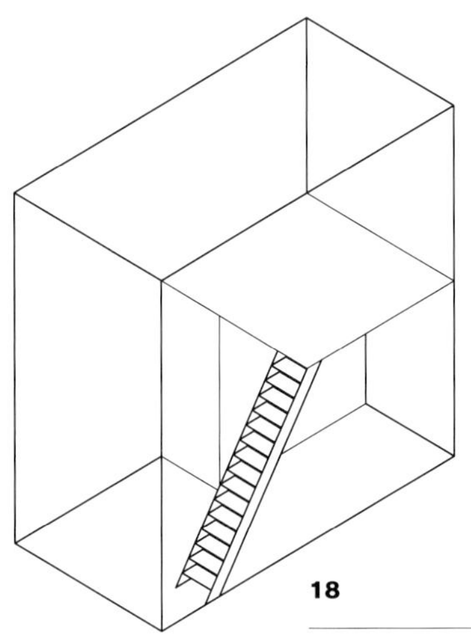

18

Finishings
Diagram of the finishing modules and elements.

19

Example of building finishing
Finishing elements in existing buildings: suspended ceilings with inspection hatches, double floors and connections ready for a system partition wall consisting of flexible modules.

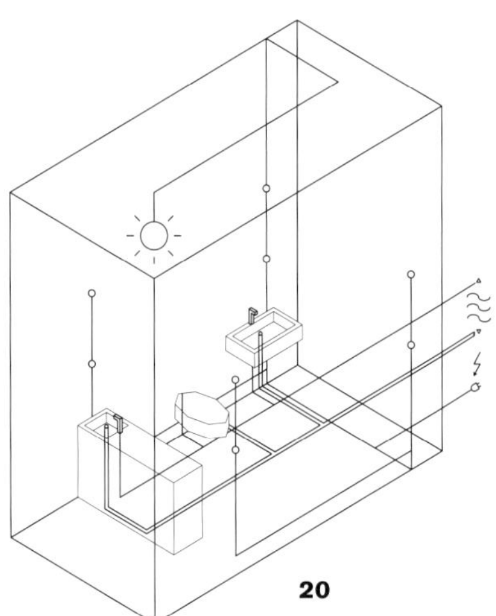

20

Building services
Diagram of integrated building services elements in the building.

21

Example of building services
Installation space: suspended ceiling with ventilation ducts, sprinkler pipes and electrical cabling.

Degree of prefabrication of the construction

As already described above, the system, modules and elements can be differentiated from one another, or the building can be divided in accordance with the work packages based on the trades involved in its construction. For both approaches the degree of prefabrication varies according to the industrial standard, technological situation and the desired degree of flexibility.

The mega-unit façade is a complete contrast to a façade made from bricks, with their small dimensions and their requirement for large amounts of skilled work on site: these façades perform all the functions of the envelope, including sealing, insulation and climatisation, and arrive on site as prefabricated modules consisting of multiple elements, requiring only to be lifted and fixed in their final positions (22). As a completely prefabricated façade, it is installed as a module of a secondary system façade. The price of complexity is reduced flexibility of the module, as adjustments or modifications on site are impossible or can only be undertaken with difficulty or to the detriment of quality.

When considering the industrial manufacture of the component materials and the incorporated elements, there is also the question of what is the ideal amount of prefabrication of the modules and elements for a particular building project. The following aspects influence the decision about the degree of prefabrication: the tradition in that section of the construction industry – what can the contractors supply, in which manufacturing processes does their experience lie? This largely defines the cost of production and therefore the price. Another relevant factor is the relationship of labour rates to material costs. In established industrialised societies with high wage costs, for reasons of economy the tendency is to reduce the labour content of a site operation to a minimum and rely upon a larger degree of prefabrication, while newly industrialised countries with low wage costs can afford to complete more complex works on site. The degree of development of the industry also has an influence; the transport costs of a complex technology that is not available locally and therefore must be imported mean it is usually too expensive to adopt. Finally, the available transport options have an influence on prefabrication. If there is no way of transporting large objects, then elements will be used instead of whole components; if on the other hand there is the option of moving whole modules or secondary systems by road or even a complete primary system, for example by ship or barge, then the idea of assembling elements into subsystems in the factory becomes more appealing.

Examples of the various stages of prefabrication of elements, modules and systems are discussed below: concrete components can be precast in formwork (23). The building only takes form on the site, but the components are manufactured in the factory. This gives flexibility of production albeit with the consequent amount of work on site.

On the other hand, masonry represents a first step towards prefabrication as the blocks or bricks have already been fabricated when they arrive on site. However, the wall is still built manually on site. The same applies to large-format wall elements, for example precast concrete units, which can perform some but not all the functions of a wall.

22

Mega-unit façade
The façade units consist of structural grid width and storey height façade modules that perform all the functions of the façade. These units are prefabricated in the factory and merely installed on site.

A next step towards prefabrication is the use of modules, i.e. components consisting of several elements and capable of performing various functions. Façade modules are an example of this. If the modules are small enough, they can be easily transported and installed. Larger modules may not be capable of being installed manually but must be lifted and placed mechanically (24).

A further step in the direction of complete prefabrication is the installation of large-format modules or whole secondary systems. In addition to the above-mentioned window modules and façade modules (25, 26), a further example is a complete roof construction prefabricated with all the functional components of the fit-out elements except for the final layer of roof tiles and installed on site (27). Here as well, the division of the modules is

23

Holiday development, Burgh-Haamstede, the Netherlands, 2003
Precasting a floor slab with edge formwork, reinforcement and in-situ concrete.

24

Holiday development, Burgh-Haamstede
Precast concrete units for walls and ceilings are a good example of large-format modular construction.

25

Holiday development, Burgh-Haamstede
Creation of the wall module with the precast concrete, insulation and masonry cladding elements. Modules such as windows are installed as the wall is being built in this form of construction.

26

Holiday development, Burgh-Haamstede
Detailed section of the wall construction with the precast concrete unit elements as loadbearing wall, insulation and masonry as the external skin, and the window module.

governed by transport requirements, as the complete roof would not be transportable on minor roads. Additional fit-out items, such as dormers, are also prefabricated, delivered and installed in the same way (28–30).

The possibility of installation of whole secondary systems largely depends on the dimensions of the modules, which still have to be transportable by road. The above-mentioned mega-unit façades and the façades of Dutch housing, such as the development in Ypenburg (31–33), are examples of this. Completely prefabricated façades are installed on to an in-situ or prefabricated concrete loadbearing structure and only require to be linked to one another at the connection points. The external skin is attached in a further step.

27

Holiday development, Burgh-Haamstede
The roof secondary system, consisting of three elements, forms a roof surface, with only the final weather-proofing layer of roof tiles to be added.

28

Holiday development, Burgh-Haamstede
Roof dormer module as a prefabricated component.

29

Holiday development, Burgh-Haamstede
The roof dormers are connected to the structural components of the roof construction. The outermost layer of roof tiles conceals the connection and seals the roof.

30

Holiday development, Burgh-Haamstede
Completed holiday home.

31

Residential development, Ypenburg, The Hague, 2008
In-situ concrete cross-wall construction constructed using storey-height mobile formwork systems, which allows a whole room to be created in one process.

32

Residential development, Ypenburg
Concrete cross-wall construction with prefabricated façades as a secondary system.

33

Residential development, Ypenburg
The prefabricated wooden façade is delivered to site. Easily recognisable are the preinstalled seals at the top horizontal edge of the window.

Maximal prefabrication is achieved when the whole primary system of the building is preinstalled in a factory and merely put in place on site (34–37). With few exceptions whole buildings cannot be prefabricated because of their size and transport problems, and therefore they are subdivided into small transportable units. It is self-evident that systems with a high degree of prefabrication do not allow much scope for adjustments on site – all units must be made to match each other and manufacturing tolerances accommodated before delivery to site. Their advantages are speed of erection and the simple reuse of the transport equipment for the whole units, as all that is required to be completed on site is the connection.

34

Apartment block, Almere, the Netherlands, Han Slavik, 1994
An apartment block constructed from containers in the experimental housing development "De Realiteijt", Almere, the Netherlands.

35

Production line De Meeuw, Eindhoven, the Netherlands, 2008
Production of residential and office containers in a process resembling an assembly line.

The division of the building into systems (primary and secondary systems), modules and elements described here makes it possible to subdivide complex buildings into smaller units and therefore organise the work according to considerations of construction and function. Functions influence the system through their superimposition – should the wall only seal and insulate or also store energy, be transparent and carry loads? The more complex the requirements placed on the building, the more complex the requirements placed on the components. The same applies to the sizes of the components, as here the issues of transport and installation have to be resolved.

36

Spacebox, student accommodation, Delft, the Netherlands, 2004
Spacebox units are manufactured and supplied as complete units by Holland Composite.

37

Mobile Home, USA
The maximum dimensions of the building are determined by its ability to be transported by road. The units are connected together on site.

Connections

The assembly of a building's system – the primary system, secondary system, modules and components – comprises the connections and the connected (40–42). The modules are separated from one another for transport at the points of connection. The connections may be integrated parts of the modules or independent connecting parts, and are designed to enable quick and easy assembly on the building site. The challenge is to make complex connections work in simple ways.

The interchangeability of building components is essential to the overall design of a product of mass customisation. The mass production and the industrial manufacture of system components is a great asset to the building market if there is a choice of component size and type. This way, a building design can be developed with more variables, but the design of the details, among them the connections, remains constant. A typical office building, for example, could require modules with fixed windows, operable windows, ventilation grilles and solid panels in various sizes.

The primary components of a building consist of basic forms – point, line, plane and volume. The connections they require generally take on the form of the component and its contact surfaces, usually nodal, linear or planar (38, 39). The hinge connection of a skeletal frame is nodal, the edge connection of a concrete wall to the floor slab is linear.

The connections vary in intention and function – they may be stiff, hinged, waterproof, airtight and flexible – and this accounts for the variety of materials such as steel, aluminium, glue or wood. The types or functions of structural connections are important when considering not only the material, but the design of the connection. Steel, with its high strength, is common as a connector for many elements of relatively brittle, elastic or weak materials. Steel connections for wood, concrete and glass are stronger than the connected material itself. They are also relatively small and require little labour time. For instance, wood connections such as ledgers for beam support, are bigger and more labour-intensive than their steel replacements.

38

Lego, game of cards and Tinkertoy

Whether for nodal, linear or planar components, connections take on many forms: laying (Lego) bricks, joining slabs with Charles and Ray Eames's House of Cards, connecting a skeletal structure with Tinkertoys.

39

Types of connections
Brickwork (nodal components with linear connections) at Tate Modern, London, Herzog & de Meuron, 2000; hollow wood panel construction of homes (planar components with linear connections) in Oxley Woods, Rogers Stirk Harbour + Partners, 2008; and detail of Stansted Airport roof structure (linear components with nodal connections), Norman Foster, 1991.

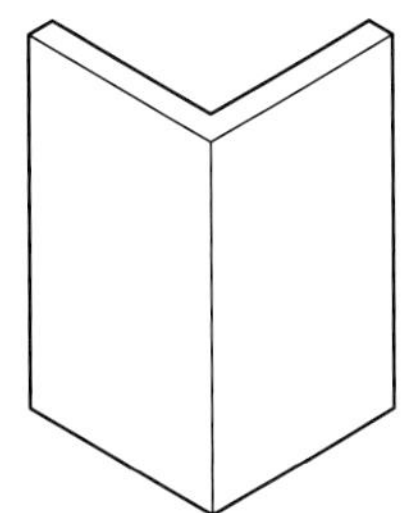
Connections wall – wall

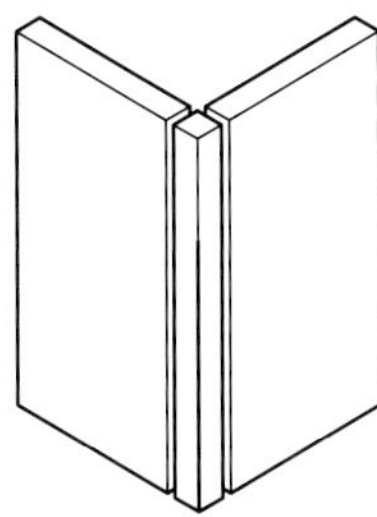
Skeletal structure

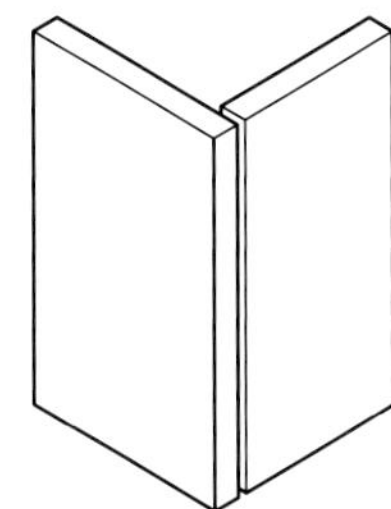
Wall panels

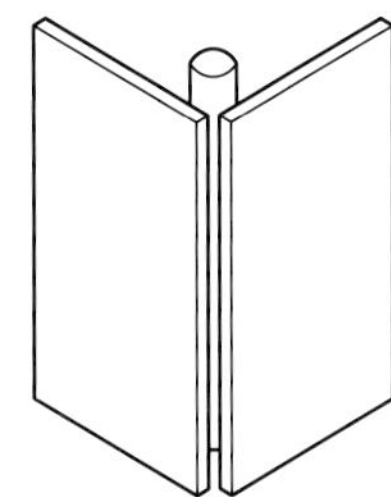
"Domino" system

Timber frame construction

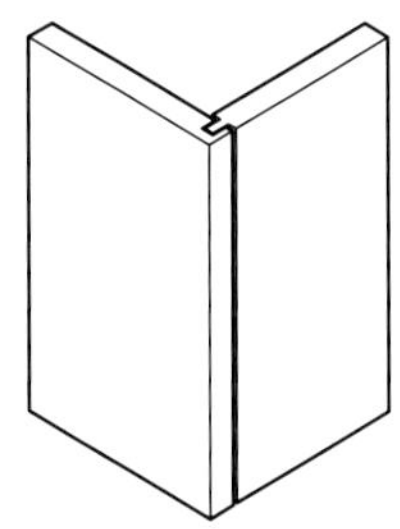
Wood or concrete panel construction

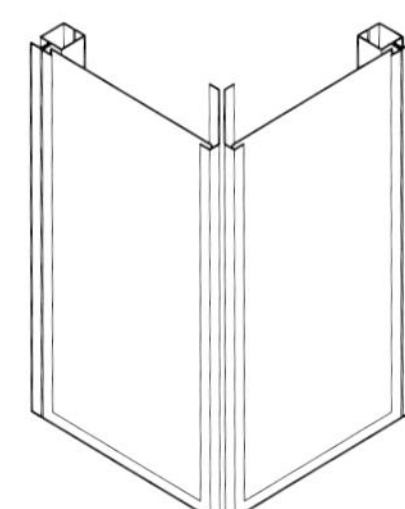
Wall panel system

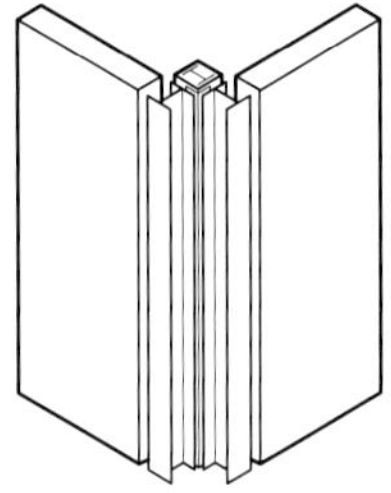
Steel skeleton structure with prefabricated panels

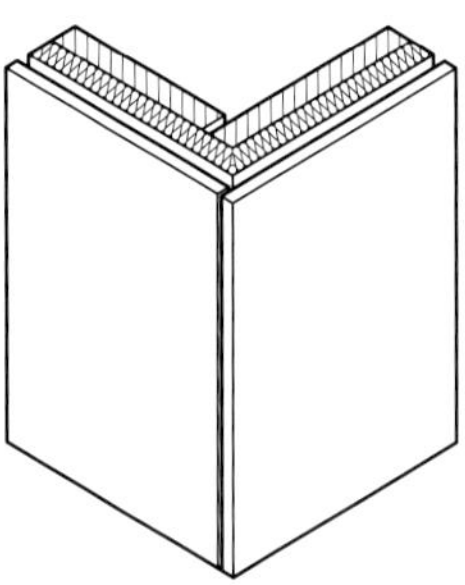
Prefabricated panels

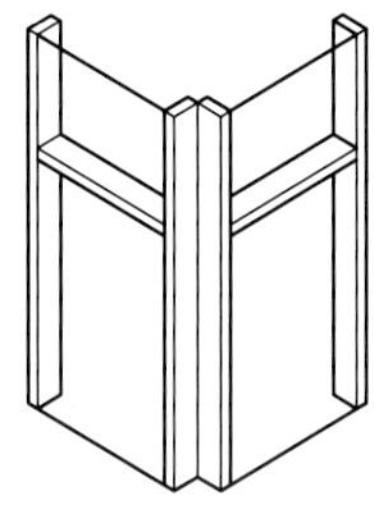
Post-and-beam construction

40

Wall-to-wall connections
In the basic examples shown here, the connection between two panels can be integrated with a primary system (the skeletal structure) or be independent of the primary system either with or without structural qualities. Le Corbusier's "domino" system, for example, involves a simple connection between suspended panels, whereas loadbearing framed panels or massive slabs involve structurally sound connections. Tolerances, fastening strengths and methods vary accordingly.

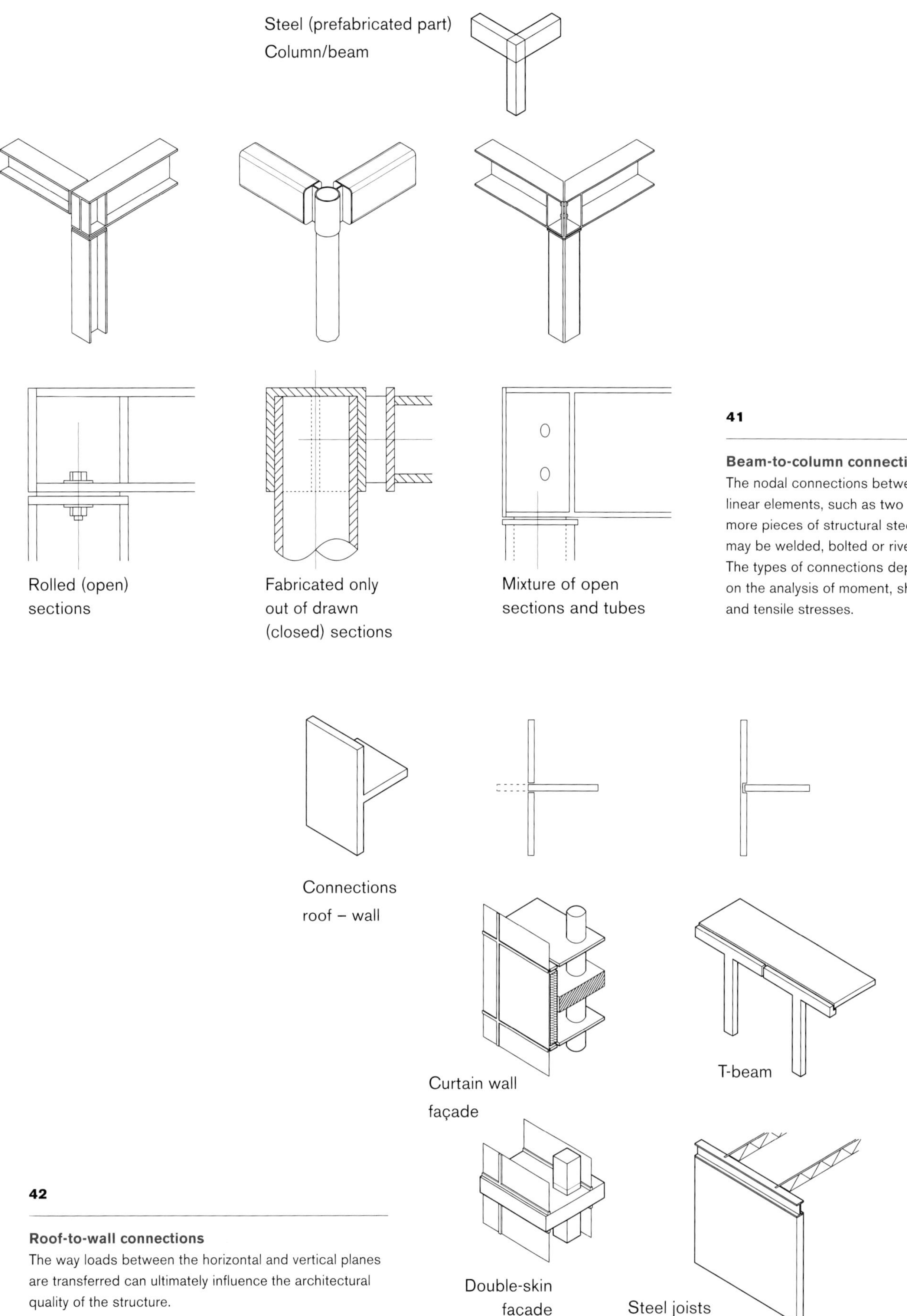

41

Beam-to-column connections
The nodal connections between linear elements, such as two or more pieces of structural steel, may be welded, bolted or riveted. The types of connections depend on the analysis of moment, shear and tensile stresses.

42

Roof-to-wall connections
The way loads between the horizontal and vertical planes are transferred can ultimately influence the architectural quality of the structure.

7 | Future of Building Systems

Building systems have come a long way, and there is a long road ahead. The logistics of building systems and the development of materials and building components have followed the progression of the building industry and shaped the design of homes, offices and cities built today. Increasingly, both the architect and the global individual are becoming aware of issues that have been neglected along the way: the conservation of the earth's natural resources and the need to plan our built environment in an intelligent and conscious way.

There are many reasons why building with systems can be the obvious choice: cost savings, quality control, construction speed and economy of materials, to name a few. Financial risk for the manufacturer and the lack of trust in factory production are two of the reasons the establishment of building with systems has been slow, laborious and abortive. The gradual understanding of materials, the design of construction and technical processes, for example, have replaced mere visions with new milestones in architecture. Where the trends in industrial building are headed is directly related to the needs and desires made available through these developments, and vice versa: it is in constant development.

The classic argument against building with prefabricated systems of elements and modules is predictable: a building is a long-term investment that warrants an individual design solution generally not associated with the repetition of prefabrication – something that one might readily accept for short- or middle-term investments. A counterpoint is the wide acceptance of automobiles, which do include interchangeable parts, although the product belongs to the category of middle- or long-term investments.

A clearly decisive factor for the outcome of system building is the price of labour. The necessity of industrialisation is defined by the cost of labour, especially of the trained workers in the building industry. For industrialised countries, the option of systemised building is advantageous. Foreign labour is imported, or work is outsourced to cheaper production locations. Highly skilled operatives are gradually becoming too expensive for use in system building on site in the developing and emerging market countries; in this context, their skills are more effectively employed in the technical development of components in the factory.

System building industry

The automobile industry made a breakthrough in the history of rationalisation and industrial efficiency with the novel development of the assembly line over 100 years ago. This was followed by improved forms of efficiency, which were responsible for the immense success of the automobile industry by implementing the individualisation of the product. Decades later, the building industry has not come close to this level of prefabrication or even mass production. Automobiles now drive faster, more smoothly, provide seemingly all comforts and are more energy-efficient. In contrast, the establishment of prefabrication in the housing, industrial and office building sectors has had only partial success. Ongoing attempts from architects, whether motivated by the search for alternative aesthetic forms or for solutions to specific problems, give impulse to the industry and prove that the desire exists.

1

Mechanical systems
The use of prefabricated elements in mechanical building systems is common practise.

Architect vs. system building

Just by observing the built environment, it becomes clear that most buildings were not designed by architects. In fact, many of the buildings built without the professional help of an architect did not require it, because they were built with prefabricated building systems that included all necessary calculations and authorisations as part of the package (1, 2). Industrial buildings need only work out their functional organisation, and fool-proof designs take care of the rest. In North America, for example, less than 5 % of all homeowners have spoken to an architect; in Europe the percentage, depending on the country, is 15–50 %.

Almost all other buildings in the residential sector are built by developers – employing a sensible use of standardisations both in terms of logistics and economics (3, 4). This automatically implies a uniformity of the homes as well as the use of industrial production. The built product also must have good marketability, meaning that any experiments with the outward appearance of

2

Simple façade system
Individualised prefabrication of large façade components.

3

Different stages of construction on a large-scale building site
Construction of a concrete structure: assemble formwork, place reinforcement, pour concrete, remove formwork.

the house can easily lead to financial disaster for a housing developer. Considering the breadth of investment a developer brings into such a project, this is too much of a risk to take. So, the decision to go stylistically mainstream is a sensible one but consequently limits any creative innovation. The alternative marketing strategy could be the branding of a fashionable theme, for example, the energy-efficient house, or the attachment of a specific branding.

The developer's marketing stance, however, does not necessarily promote architectural quality nor does it call for the architect's creativity. Given the low profit margin of individually designed and manufactured buildings, the resulting low profit margins of all involved and high prices of materials to top it off, the development toward a stronger standardisation is an advantage for all parties. While most architects use digital design tools, they are often hesitant to adopt a digitally governed building construction process: they are afraid this would have detrimental effects and result in a uniform manufactured product by limiting their control over the detailing.

4

EnBV City, Stuttgart, RKW Architektur + Städtebau, 2008
The logistics of a large construction site must accommodate various simultaneous building stages. For increased efficiency, the upper floors of the building structure are still under construction while in the lower areas the façade panels are already being mounted.

CAD and CAM

A challenging issue today is the individualisation of systemised building (6). The experience with overly uniform housing developments, the resulting social problems and, in the worst case, its uselessness, has left system building with a stigma. At the same time, building must respect the individual needs of the society. With the implementation of CAD (computer-aided design) systems, it is possible to resolve these problems using mass customisation. Tools for administering data, organising and processing were accordingly developed and are key in the planning process (5). CAD programmes are also developed for the logistics of supplier coordination, production, transportation and assembly. CAM (computer-aided manufacturing) directly translates the design to the product, cutting study models as well as producing elements and modules. Its application in more complex building systems is, however, less present.

Today it is evident that the full switch from paper to CAD architectural drawings and partly to CAM systems has taken place with improvements in the quality of building construction (6). The coordination of the interface between design, fabrication and assembly, which is necessary in achieving building construction completely controlled by CAD/CAM systems, is still in continuous development.

Digital Age

We build with systems, and these systems have become more complex. We have tested almost all combinations and permutations of systems; at the same time they must be versatile enough to ride the waves of the quickly changing context of time, information and technology. The challenge is to satisfy the needs of a generation used to the constant renewal of gadgets such as mobile phones, laptops, entertainment stations or automobile extras.

Likewise, the market for building industry products was very different as little as a decade ago, and we can expect similar advancements in another ten years. Reyner Banham may have observed this with amusement, were he alive today. He defined the First Machine Age, followed by the Second Machine Age, and speculated over the Third Machine Age, which was all about mobility and experience – as presented by his colleagues at Archigram, Superstudio and Haus Rucker Co. with the futuristic Plug-In City, The Walking Machine and the Mind Expander. The Machine Age now is certainly the Digital Age, the age of limitless communication and information. The architects of the ages have consequently been building according to the ages – with practical intent in the First Machine Age, with ambitions in design in the Second Machine Age, with poetic freedom in the Third and now, with variability and choice. In the context of the Digital Age, the building industry is also aspiring to offer variability and choice.

5

Building system for a storage facility
Maximum efficiency is achieved through planning, standardisation, prefabrication, logistics and assembly.

When limits are reached, there must be a turn. Joel Garreau, analyst of global culture and author of *Edge City*, an account of the inevitable expansion of America's suburbs, identifies a few of such limits. Since the start of industrialisation, the railroad building industry has experienced 14 doublings of railroad production. The exponential curve waned off, resulting in an S-curve. Garreau applies Moore's Law to this example of industrial expansion. Named after the co-founder of Intel, the law regarding the long-term trend in the history of computing hardware states that the rate of growth of the storage capacity of a transistor, and later the chip, is increasing exponentially. From 1960 until 2004, it has experienced 27 doublings. The continuous expansion of material and knowledge must end somewhere, or the top of the S-curve is often overlapped with the beginnings of new curves. The railroad industry met with other forms of transportation. The automobile industry, which has experienced similar growth, has made cars first faster and bigger, then smaller and trendier; the work is now concentrated on electronic gadgets and lower gasoline consumption. The Digital Age must similarly reach the top of the S-curve.

The same applies to building technology. The advancements in materials and methods have far exceeded their purpose. Concrete decking can be made almost as thin as cardboard, but walking on it does not feel solid anymore. Steel buildings are made to withstand earthquakes, wind and fire and reach enormous heights but often lack usable space. We have structural glass, transparent concrete, bent wood and non-scratchable plastic. Lean production methods cannot become more efficient.

The answer to the future of building systems does not lie in improvements, as we can pretentiously admit that there are few improvements to be made. Instead we must attend to the negligence of the environment; each conscious step towards a greener environment is a challenge in creativity and technology.

6

Jin Mao Tower, Shanghai, Skidmore, Owings and Merrill, 1998
The complex façade of the Jin Mao Tower was prefabricated in Germany by Gartner and transported by ship to Shanghai, where it was installed.

Sustainable building and intelligent design

As the development of technology advances, the demands on the science of building increase. Sparked by the intensive debates on global warming and the related topics on energy-saving measures, building regulations have become stricter. The architects' increasingly urgent challenge is pre-empted by the startling fact that buildings are responsible for half of the world's CO_2 emissions and a great share of the world's energy and water consumption. Reducing a building's impact on the environment while maintaining optimum indoor comfort requires precise, well-orchestrated building and service systems of highest quality. Usage and maintenance costs affect the building's value.

The embodied energy (EE) of a building is an important consideration for architects and building owners when designing the construction of a building. Different from the operating energy (electricity, heating, cooling, etc.), which accounts for between 50–80 % of the energy consumed by a building, the EE is the cumulative energy required for all stages of the building's life: the procuring of the materials, the manufacture, transportation and recycling. The use of building systems that allow for easy disassembling and recycling of components helps sustain a green environment. Furthermore, the use of reusable parts such as wall and floor panels (8) is especially useful in a world of

7

Unilever Headquarters, Hamburg, Behnisch Architekten, 2009

The double façade with outer ETFE foil layer allows for the optimised natural circulation of air and is an example of advancement in systemised building climate engineering. The use of resource-efficient technology, such as concrete core activation for cooling and a heat recovery system, achieves a primary energy requirement of only 100 kWh/a/m².

changing office patterns and demographics. The objectives of optimum flexibility, more efficient technologies, increased quality of a product and waste reduction can be greatly improved with prefabrication.

In Western Europe the aims of sustainable building have already been addressed and often been integrated into general building practice. The relatively high energy prices are an additional incentive. Furthermore, the European Union and national governments have made consistent efforts to develop sustainable building. A typical office building in Germany uses about 25 % less energy than one in the USA (7). Now, for most young architects in Western Europe, building sustainable architecture is seen as a moral responsibility. Many of the most ambitious experiments are carried out by European architects with clients seeking not only cost-saving solutions, but also a very modern corporate identity found in sustainability. Objectives of reaching 'zero energy' by balancing primary energy needs through heat and power generation as well as integrated photovoltaics are not improbable goals.

Building Information Modelling

Building Information Modelling (BIM), an open platform for use by all the design disciplines involved in a construction project, allows an integrated rather than a sectionalised approach to the design of the architecture, building services and loadbearing structure as early as at the preliminary design stage. The automobile and aerospace industries were also leaders in the development of this technique. Working with BIM synchronises the information flows of each project participant. Changes during the design process are automatically implemented in the whole project, and, as all the designers have access to the same model, the consequences are immediately apparent for all the specialist disciplines. The design process as such is systemised, and the synchronised processing and immediate checking of the data comprise new design opportunities for the architect.

8

Interior furnishings

Demountable partitions and furniture allow flexibility of working patterns without exorbitant remodelling costs and hence a prolonged use of materials.

Sustainability rating systems

In recent years governments of many nations have come up with sustainability rating systems with which architects, builders and property owners must or can comply. The LEED programme of the United States Green Building Council, for example, a non-profit group set up in 1993, the Energy Star programme also of the USA and the younger Green Star of Australia aim to promote green building practices. In Great Britain, the BRE (Building Research Establishment) has initiated BREEAM (for non-residential buildings) and Ecohomes (for residential buildings) as environmental rating schemes. The rating systems vary, but they generally take into account design, construction methods, living comfort, energy conservation, power generation, materials and recyclability in the calculation of a green building. Awards, seals, memberships and the like are voluntary but are signs of ecological quality, which facilitate the differentiation for the non-professionals and likewise increase the attractiveness of a product for the eco-minded consumer. Critics of these programmes claim that builders spend too much time collecting points for rating systems rather than concentrating on working on real solutions. All in all, however, for the building industry and the countries that have such rating systems, it is a sign of progress in the industry.

Whereas earlier buildings applied more or less standard methods of interior temperature and climate control (also known as building systems in the context of mechanical engineering) to maintain a comfortable indoor environment, today building physics are integrated into the early stages of the design. Architects are networking with climate engineers to develop specialised solutions for intelligent climate control with sustainable building methods in projects such as Harvard's Allston Science Complex (9) in Boston (design: Behnisch Architekten 2008; climate engi-

9

Harvard Allston Science Complex, Boston, Behnisch Architekten, design 2008
The design comprises an intelligent climate control system and will thus achieve an optimised overall energy performance.The building skin has moveable parts for ventilation, sun-shading and light shelves that direct light deep into laboratory spaces.

neering: Transsolar). Façade consultants and structural engineers also contribute to efficient green buildings using elements such as the building's orientation, sun shades, layered façades and natural cooling and ventilation methods (10–12). Generally, it is essential to build with the prospect that the spaces may be temporary or short-lived, but that the materials can be recycled. Prefabricated building systems are the key to recycling spaces or components.

11

Headquarters Q-Cells, Bitterfeld, Germany, bhss-architekten, 2009
The administration building was put together from six-storey office building modules. The multi-layer façade construction contains solar panels, which provide shade and generate energy.

10

SAP Call Centre, Galway, Ireland, Bucholz McEvoy Architects, 2005
The deep beams of the atrium form a herringbone pattern and are oriented towards the sun path to provide optimum light at different times of the day. Slender prefabricated façade panels house natural cross ventilation systems.

Development potential of system building

One of the fundamental lessons of this study of systems is that in order to build with a system, not all the demands and details have to be resolved within that one system of solutions. The more determining task is to resolve only the essential problems with a building system, and then to find new solutions for specific problems.

The future of building systems does not depend on better detail solutions or more efficient design of construction; the more relevant issues are:

- logistics and distribution suiting individual needs of the user, the architect and the manufacturer
- flexibility and reusability, in order to adapt to an ever-changing society for which variable and mobile systems are essential
- sustainability, renewable energy, materials and their embodied energy (EE), the ability to recycle

Despite the tendency to think that prefabricated or system building has only negative effects on the architectural profession, young professionals pursue new ways of thinking not by working against, but with the industry of building systems. With the numerous types of applications system building has for dealing with design flexibility, cost savings, quality control and sustainability, architects actually have great potential to utilise it.

12

Elm Park Development, Dublin, Bucholz McEvoy Architects, 2008
The climate-controlled buildings provide high comfort levels without the use of mechanical ventilation or air-conditioning. Prefabricated panels are oriented toward the sun for better effectivity.

Selected Bibliography

History and General Documentation

Baldwin, J.
Bucky Works: Buckminster Fuller's Ideas for Today
Wiley & Sons, New York, 1996

Banham, Reyner
Theory and Design in the First Machine Age
The Architectural Press, London, 1960

Banham, Reyner
The Architecture of the Well-Tempered Environment
The University of Chicago Press, Chicago, 1969

Banham, Reyner
"Klarheit, Ehrlichkeit, Einfachkeit … and Wit Too!: The Case Study Houses in the World's Eyes", in: Smith, Elisabeth A. T. (ed.),
Blueprints for Modern Living: History and Legacy of the Case Study Houses
MIT Press, Cambridge, Mass., 1989, p. 183–196

Bergdoll, Barry and Christensen, Peter
Home Delivery: Fabricating the Modern Dwelling
The Museum of Modern Art, New York, and Birkhäuser, Basel, 2008

Buisson, Ethel and Billard, Thomas
The Presence of the Case Study Houses
Birkhäuser, Basel, 2004

Colomina, Beatriz
"Escape from Today: Houses of the Future", in: Vegesack, Alexander von and Eisenbrand, Jochen (ed.)
Open House: Architektur und Technologie für intelligentes Wohnen
Vitra Design Museum, Weil am Rhein, 2007, p. 228–257

Davies, Colin
The Prefabricated Home
Reaktion Books, London, 2005

Futagawa, Yukio (ed.)
Paul Rudolph: Dessins d'architecture, Architekturzeichnungen, Architectural Drawings
Architectural Book Publishing, New York, 1981

Garreau, Joel
Edge City
Doubleday, New York, 1988

Hayden, Dolores
A Field Guide to Sprawl
W. W. Norton & Company, New York, 2004

Hayden, Dolores
Building Suburbia: Green Fields and Urban Growth 1820–2000
Vintage Books, New York, 2003

Head, Peter
"Entering the Ecological Age: The Engineer's Role", The Brunel Lecture, London, 2008
http://www.arup.com/_assets/_download/72B9BD7D-19BB-316E-40000ADE36037C13.pdf

Herbert, Gilbert
Pioneers of Prefabrication: The British Contribution in the 19th Century
The Johns Hopkins University Press, Baltimore, 1978

Herbert, Gilbert
The Dream of the Factory-Made House
MIT Press, Cambridge, Mass., 1984

Höpfner, Rosemarie and Fischer, Volker (ed.), commissioned by Dezernat für Kultur und Freizeit, Amt für Wissenschaft und Kunst, Stadt Frankfurt am Main
Ernst May und das Neue Frankfurt 1925–1930
Ernst und Sohn, Berlin, 1986

Jessee, Chris and Rourk, Will
The Crystal Palace: 3D Modeling
Institute for Advanced Technology in the Humanities, University of Virginia, 2001
http://www2.iath.virginia.edu/london/model/

Kaluarachchi, Y. D., Tah, J. H. M. and Howes, R.
"The Historical Development of Standardised Building Systems Associated with Social Housing in the UK", in: Journal for Housing Science, vol. 26, no. 1, 2002, p. 15–26

Kirsch, Karin
Die Weißenhofsiedlung: Werkbund-Ausstellung DIE WOHNUNG Stuttgart 1927
Deutsche Verlagsanstalt Stuttgart, 1987, 2nd edition 1999

Le Corbusier
Toward an Architecture
Los Angeles, Getty Research Institute, 2007

McCoy, Esther
Case Study Houses 1945–1962
Hennessey & Ingalls, Santa Monica, California, 1977
(first published in 1962 under the title Modern California Houses)

McCoy, Esther and Goldstein, Barbara (ed.)
Arts & Architecture: The Entenza Years
Columbia Lithograph, Santa Fe Springs, California, 1990
(selective reprint of Arts & Architecture from 1943–1959)

"Measures in Japanese Culture", in:
Kansai Window
http://www.kippo.or.jp/culture_e/build/measure.html

Pawley, Martin
The Private Future
Random House, New York, 1974

Pawley, Martin
"A Prefab Future", in: Grant, Carol (ed.),
Built to Last? Reflections on British Housing Policy. A Collection of Articles from ROOF Magazine
The Russell Press, Nottingham, 1989 (reprinted in 1994), p. 77–84

Phillipson, Mark
"Defining the Sustainability of Prefabrication and Modular Process in Construction"
Building Research Establishment, Garston, 2003
http://projects.bre.co.uk/prefabrication/prefabrication.pdf

Russell, Barry
Building Systems, Industrialization and Architecture
Wiley & Sons, New York, 1981

Smith, Elizabeth
Case Study Houses
Taschen, Cologne, 2006

Smithson, Alison and Peter
Changing the Art of Inhabitation
Artemis London, London, 1994

Steinhausen, Ansgar
"Plattenbau. Eine architekturhistorische Darstellung", in: DAM Architektur Jahrbuch
Prestel, Munich, 1994, p. 25–38

Stevenson, Katherine Cole and Jandl, H. Ward
Houses by Mail: A Guide to Houses from Sears, Roebuck and Company
Wiley & Sons, New York, 1986

Vidotto, Marco
Alison and Peter Smithson: Works and Projects
Ingoprint, Barcelona, 1997

Wachsmann, Konrad, Grüning, Michael, Grüning, Christa and Sumi, Christian
Building the Wooden House.
Technique and Design
Birkhäuser, Basel, 1995 (first published in German in 1930)

Whiteley, Nigel
The Digital Age: the Fourth Machine Age, 2005
http://www.a4a.info/viza/html/v-018-01.html

Housing

Arieff, Allison and Burkhart, Bryan
Prefab
Gibbs Smith, Layton, Utah, 2002

Brown, Karen A. et al
"Quadrant Homes Applies Lean Concepts in a Project Environment",
in: Goliath Business News, 2004
http://goliath.ecnext.com/coms2/gi_0199-4859154/Quadrant-Homes-applies-lean-concepts.html

Ching, Francis D. K.
Building Construction Illustrated
Wiley & Sons, New York, 4th edition 2008

dieGesellschafter.de, "So wohnt Deutschland"
http://diegesellschafter.de/information/dossiers/dossier.php?did=28&z1=1261260575&z2=cb67d7d750ee3141b4184efe8f4fa6b9&

Egan, Sir John
Rethinking Construction:
Report of the Construction Task Force
HMSO, London, 1998

"Factory and Site-Built Housing: A Comparison for the 21st Century", in: ToolBase Services, 1998
http://www.toolbase.org/Construction-Methods/Manufactured-Housing/factory-site-built-comparison

Hoke, John Ray (ed.)
Ramsey/Sleeper Architectural Graphic Standards
Wiley & Sons, New York, 11th edition 2007

Hönig, Roderick, "Fertighaus nach Mass", in:
NZZ-Folio, 2002
http://www.nextroom.at/article.php?x=y&article_id=1275

Knutt, Elaine
"Is the Prefab Revolution on Hold?",
in: Building Design, February 3, 2006
http://www.bdonline.co.uk/story.asp?storyCode=3062135

Mathieu, Renee
"The Prefabricated Housing Industries in the United States, Sweden and Japan",
in: Construction Review, July/August 1987
http://findarticles.com/p/articles/mi_m3035/is_v33/ai_5221728/?tag=content;col1

Shelar, Scott
"Labor Shortage Threatening U. S. Construction Industry"
in: Atlanta Business Chronicle, 1997
http://www.bizjournals.com/atlanta/stories/1997/09/08/focus17.html

"Whole-House Systems",
in: ToolBase Services, 2007
http://www.toolbase.org/ToolbaseResources/level3.aspx?BucketID=1&CategoryID=13

Industrial Buildings

Beyeler, Theresia, Medici, Roberto and Office Haller
Catalogue for exhibition
"Fritz Haller Bauen und Forschen"
Office Fritz Haller, Solothurn, 1998

Broeze, Frank
The Globalisation of the Oceans
International Maritime Economic History Association, St. Johns, Newfoundland, 2002

"Elemente und Systeme" (special issue)
DETAIL, no. 4, 2001

"Haus der Zukunft"
ARCH+, no. 198/199, 2010

Köhler, Lutz
Entwicklungen beim Bau von Produktionsgewächshäusern
Institute for Technology in Garden Construction, Weihenstephan University of Applied Sciences, 2002

"Leichtbau und Systeme" (special issue)
DETAIL, no. 7/8, 2006

Lichtenberg, Jos
Slimbouwen
Aenaes, uitgeverij van vakinformatie, Boxtel, 2005

Staib, Gerald, Dörrhöfer, Andreas and Rosenthal, Markus
Components and Systems: Modular Construction.
Design, Structure, New Technologies
Edition Detail, Munich, and Birkhäuser, Basel, 2008

Wichmann, Hans and Haller, Fritz
System-Design: Fritz Haller.
Bauten – Möbel – Forschung
Birkhäuser, Basel, 1989

Witthöft, Hans Jürgen
Container. Die Mega-Carrier kommen
Koehler, Hamburg, 2nd edition 2004

Wachsmann, Konrad
Wendepunkt im Bauen
Krausskopf Verlag, Wiesbaden, 1959

Processes

Ford, Henry and Crowther, Samuel
Today and Tomorrow
Productivity Press, Detroit, 1988
(first published in 1926)

Gundermann, Beate
Schlüsselfertiges Bauen: Logistik im Ausbau bei schlüsselfertiger Bauausführung
Thesis, Dortmund University, 1997

Knaack, Ulrich and Hasselbach, Reinhard
New Strategies for Systems
Delft University of Technology, Delft 2006

Liker, Jeffrey K.
The Toyota Way
McGraw Hill, New York, 2004

Mainka, Thomas
Rationalisierungsreserven in der schlüsselfertigen Bauausführung
Doctoral thesis, Dortmund University, 1986

Ohno, Taiichi
Toyota Production System:
Beyond Large-Scale Production
Productivity Press, Detroit, 1988

Womack, James P., Jones, Daniel T. and Roos, Daniel
The Machine That Changed the World
Harper Perennial, New York, 1991

Components

Ackermann, Kurt
Tragwerke in der konstruktiven Architektur
Deutsche Verlagsanstalt, Stuttgart, 1988

Ackermann, Kurt
Geschossbauten für Gewerbe und Industrie,
Deutsche Verlagsanstalt, Stuttgart, 1993

Boake, Terri Meyer
Unterstanding Steel Design:
An Architectural Design Manual
Birkhäuser, Basel, 2012

Bräm, Matthias
Konstruktives Entwerfen mit Betonelementen
ZWH Zurich University of Applied Sciences,
Winterthur, 2002

Braun, Dietrich, "Phantastisch Plastisch",
in: Blücher, Claudia von and Erdmann, Günther
et al (ed.)
Faszination Kunststoff
Deutsches Kunststoff Museum, Düsseldorf, 1998

Hauschild, Moritz
Konstruieren im Raum:
Eine Baukonstruktionslehre zum Studium
Callwey, Munich, 2003

Krieg, Stefan
"Gusseiserne Elementbauten",
in: DAM Architektur Jahrbuch
Prestel, Munich, 1994, p. 11–23

Rush, Richard D. (ed.)
The Building Systems Integration Handbook
Butterworth-Heinemann, Stoneham, Mass., 1986
(reprinted 1991)

"Steel and You: The Life of Steel",
International Iron and Steel Institute,
Bruxelles, 2008
http://www.worldsteel.org/?action=publicationdetail&id=71

Trewin, Ed
The Advanced Composites Industry:
Global Markets, Technology Trends and
Applications 2002–2007
Materials Technology Publications, Watford, 2003

Watts, Andrew
Modern Construction Handbook
Springer, Vienna, 2009

Useful Websites

Fabprefab – modernist prefab dwellings
http://www.fabprefab.com/fabfiles/fablisthome.htm

Inhabitat
http://www.inhabitat.com/category/architecture/

dwell modern home magazine online
http://www.dwell.com/articles/101-prefab.html

Some Assembly Required: Contemporary
Prefabricated Houses
http://design.walkerart.org/prefab

Authors

Professor Dr. Ing. Ulrich Knaack is an architect and worked in an architectural practice in Düsseldorf. Today, he is Professor for Design of Construction and Building Technology at the Delft University of Technology, the Netherlands; he is also Professor for Design and Construction at Ostwestfalen-Lippe University of Applied Sciences in Detmold, Germany. He is author of several well-known reference books on glass in architecture and editor of the publication series Principles of Construction.

Dipl.-Ing. Sharon Chung-Klatte is an architect with degrees from Cornell University and the Kunstakademie Düsseldorf, where she earned the title "Meisterschülerin". She worked in practices in New York, London and Germany, among them the offices of Oswald Mathias Ungers and Ingenhoven, Overdiek und Partner. She has taught architectural design and construction at various universities, including the Akademie van Bouwkunst Maastricht in the Netherlands, the Kunstakademie Düsseldorf and Ostwestfalen-Lippe University of Applied Sciences in Detmold, Germany. She is currently practicing in Düsseldorf.

Dipl.-Ing. Reinhard Hasselbach studied architecture at RWTH Aachen. System building is the focus of his research, which he undertakes at the chair of Professor Knaack at the Delft University of Technology, the Netherlands. He is a practicing architect and curator in Berlin.

Index

Page numbers in italics refer to images.

Illustration Credits

1 Introduction
1, 4, 8 Sharon Chung-Klatte
2, 7, 9 Ulrich Knaack
3 Ben Parco
5, 6 Rieder Faserbeton-Elemente GmbH

2 History of Building Systems
1 Martin Schumann
2 Museum of Fine Arts, Boston
4 from: Bernard Rudofsky, Architecture Without Architects, Museum of Modern Art, New York, 1964
5 Mark Boucher
6, 26, 27 from: Walter Meyer-Bohe, Vorfertigung, Vulkan-Verlag Dr. W. Classen, Essen, 1964, S. 29, 170
7 Anja Krämer, Freunde der Weißenhof-siedlung e. V.
8 Holger Ellgard
9 Klemens Erdmann
10 from: Frank D. Graham and Thomas J. Emery, Audel's Carpenter's and Builder's Guide, T. Audel & Co, New York, 1923 (reprints 1947, 1951)
11 National Archives and Records Administration, Washington
12, 13 Sears Brands, LLC
14, 19, 39 Sharon Chung-Klatte
17, 18 Dr. Paul Wolff & Tritschler, Institut für Stadtgeschichte, Frankfurt am Main
20 Bauhaus Stiftung
21 Staatsgalerie Stuttgart, Graphische Sammlung
23, 35, 41 Ulrich Knaack
24 Dominique Zehrfuss-Modiano, Cité de l'Architecture et du Patrimonie, Centre d'Archives d'Architecture, Cité Chaillot
25 photograph: Jean-Luc Valentin, Stefan Forster Architekten
26 Zoe Star Small
32, 33 Crown, National Monuments Record
37 Denise McKinney
38 Fred Hong
42, 44 The Estate of R. Buckminster Fuller
45, 47 archive Konrad Wachsmann, Akademie der Künste Berlin
48, 49 Reinhard Hasselbach
50, 51 Smithson Family Collection
52, 53 Library of Congress, Prints and Photographs Division

3 Systems in Housing
3, 4, 5, 26 Tae Hyun Chung
7 Marcel Bilow
8, 15, 21, 31, 32 Ulrich Knaack
9, 10, 11, 16, 17, 24 Oskar Leo Kaufmann and Albert Ruf with Johannes Kaufmann
12 Penny Collins and Huw Turner
13 Simpson Strong-Tie Company Inc.
18, 19 John Ware
20 red fur ball, Flickr
22 Reinhard Hasselbach
27 Jay David
28 Anderson Anderson Architecture
29 Alchemy Architects
33 Toyota Homes
34, 35 F.O.B. Architecture and F.O.B. Homes
36 photograph: Tony Maclean, Rogers Stirk Harbour + Partners
37, 39, 40 Sharon Chung-Klatte
38 Ignacio Martinez

4 Systems in Industrial Buildings
4, 5, 6 Zendome
8, 9, 12 Containex
13 photograph: Roland Tännler
14 De Meeuw
19 ERNE AG Holzbau, Laufenburg
20, 21, 22 Haller Bauen und Forschen, Therese Beyeler
25 photograph: Christiaan de Bruijne, OTH – Ontwerpgroep Trude Hooykaas
26 photograph: Gido Wesdorp
27, 30 Goldbeck
31 iStockphoto.com/Baloncici
32 CD20 Bouwsystemen
33 Fischer Bauplanung
34 Ballmoos Krucker Architekten
35, 36, 37, 38, 39 TU Delft, Jürgen Heinzel

5 Processes
3, 4 Ford-Werke
9 iStockphoto.com/archives
10, 11 Reinhard Hasselbach
12, 15, 16 DW Systembau
13, 14 Goldbeck
17 Haller Bauen und Forschen, Therese Beyeler
18 Reinhard Hasselbach, De Meeuw

6 The Components: Systems, Modules and Elements
1, 3, 6, 7, 14, 19, 21, 22, 23, 24, 25, 26, 27, 28, 29, 30, 31, 32, 33, 34, 35, 36, 37 Ulrich Knaack
2, 15, 17 Marcel Bilow
38, 39 Sharon Chung-Klatte

7 Future of Building Systems
1, 3, 4, 5 Ulrich Knaack
2, 7 Marcel Bilow
6 photographs: Richard Schieferle, Josef Gartner GmbH
8 Hanns Joosten
9 Behnisch Architekten
10, 12 Michael Moran
11 bhss-architekten

We are especially grateful to these image providers. All other illustrations were created specifically for this book or were provided by the authors. Every reasonable attempt has been made to identify owners of copyright. If unintentional mistakes or omissions occurred, we sincerely apologise and ask for a short notice. Such mistakes will be corrected in the next edition of this publication.

Façades
Principles of Construction
Ulrich Knaack; Tillmann Klein; Marcel Bilow; Thomas Auer

Introduction on the principles of faade design and construction for practitioners and students

135 pages. 165 ills., 140 drawings
21.0 x 27.0 cm. Softcover.

ISBN 978-3-7643-7962-9

Facade Construction Manual
Thomas Herzog; Roland Krippner; Werner Lang

This new first edition of the Facade Construction Manual provides a systematic survey of contemporary expertise in the application of n materials and energy- efficient technologies in facade design, and r resentsan invaluable addition to our series of Construction Manual

319 pages. 350 colour, 50 b/w ills and 500 drawings
23.0 x 29.7 cm. Hardcover.

ISBN 978-3-7643-7109-8

Constructing Architecture
Materials, Processes, Structures, A Handbook
Andrea Deplazes, ETH Zurich, Switzerland (Ed.)

Combining creativity and technical expertise: an integral approach to design and construction

512 pages. 610 ills, 920 plans and drawings
23.5 x 29.7 cm. Softcover

ISBN 978-3-7643-7189-0

Birkhäuser
P.O. Box
CH-4009 Basel

BIRKHÄUSER